D1482197

LAST WILLS MADE E-Z!

E·Z LEGAL FORMS®

Deerfield Beach, Florida
www.e-zlegal.com

00-2233

Last Wills Made E-Z™
Copyright 1999 E-Z Legal Forms, Inc.
Printed in the United States of America

E·Z LEGAL FORMS®

384 South Military Trail Deerfield Beach, FL 33442
Tel. 954-480-8933 Fax 954-480-8906
http://www.e-zlegal.com/
All rights reserved.
Distributed by E-Z Legal Forms, Inc.

1 2 3 4 5 6 7 8 9 10   CPC   R 10 9 8 7 6 5 4 3 2

This publication is designed to provide accurate and authoritative information in regard to subject matter covered. It is sold with the understanding that neither the publisher nor author is engaged in rendering legal, accounting, or other professional services. If legal advice or other expert assistance is required, the services of a competent professional should be sought. From: *A Declaration of Principles jointly adopted by a Committee of the American Bar Association and a Committee of Publishers.*

Last Wills Made E-Z™

Everyone needs a will

1

Limited warranty and disclaimer

This self-help legal product is intended to be used by the consumer for his/her own benefit. It may not be reproduced in whole or in part, resold or used for commercial purposes without written permission from the publisher. In addition to copyright violations, the unauthorized reproduction and use of this product to benefit a second party may be considered the unauthorized practice of law.

This product is designed to provide authoritative and accurate information in regard to the subject matter covered. However, the accuracy of the information is not guaranteed, as laws and regulations may change or be subject to differing interpretations. Consequently, you may be responsible for following alternative procedures, or using material or forms different from those supplied with this product. It is strongly advised that you examine the laws of your state before acting upon any of the material contained in this product.

As with any legal matter, common sense should determine whether you need the assistance of an attorney. We urge you to consult with an attorney, qualified estate planner, or tax professional, or to seek any other relevant expert advice whenever substantial sums of money are involved, you doubt the suitability of the product you have purchased, or if there is anything about the product that you do not understand including its adequacy to protect you. Even if you are completely satisfied with this product, we encourage you to have your attorney review it.

It is understood that by using this guide, you are acting as your own attorney. Neither the author, publisher, distributor nor retailer are engaged in rendering legal, accounting or other professional services. Accordingly, the publisher, author, distributor and retailer shall have neither liability nor responsibility to any party for any loss or damage caused or alleged to be caused by the use of this product.

Copyright Notice

The purchaser of this guide is hereby authorized to reproduce in any form or by any means, electronic or mechanical, including photocopying, all forms and documents contained in this guide, provided it is for nonprofit, educational or private use. Such reproduction requires no further permission from the publisher and/or payment of any permission fee.

The reproduction of any form or document in any other publication intended for sale is prohibited without the written permission of the publisher. Publication for nonprofit use should provide proper attribution to E-Z Legal Forms.

Money-back guarantee

E-Z Legal Forms offers you a limited guarantee. If you consider this product to be defective or in any way unsuitable you may return this product to us within 30 days from date of purchase for a full refund of the list or purchase price, whichever is lower. This return must be accompanied by a dated and itemized sales receipt. In no event shall our liability—or the liability of any retailer— exceed the purchase price of the product. Use of this product constitutes

Important Notice

Table of contents

How to use this guide

E-Z Legal's Made E-Z™ Guides can help you achieve an important legal objective conveniently, efficiently and economically. But it is important to properly use this guide if you are to avoid later difficulties.

◆ Carefully read all information, warnings and disclaimers concerning the legal forms in this guide. If after thorough examination you decide that you have circumstances that are not covered by the forms in this guide, or you do not feel confident about preparing your own documents, consult an attorney.

◆ Complete each blank on each legal form. Do not skip over inapplicable blanks or lines intended to be completed. If the blank is inapplicable, mark "N/A" or "None" or use a dash. This shows you have not overlooked the item.

◆ Always use pen or type on legal documents—never use pencil.

◆ Avoid erasures and "cross-outs" on final documents. Use photocopies of each document as worksheets, or as final copies. All documents submitted to the court must be printed on one side only.

◆ Correspondence forms may be reproduced on your own letterhead if you prefer.

◆ Whenever legal documents are to be executed by a partnership or corporation, the signatory should designate his or her title.

◆ It is important to remember that on legal contracts or agreements between parties all terms and conditions must be clearly stated. Provisions may not be enforceable unless in writing. All parties to the agreement should receive a copy.

◆ Instructions contained in this guide are for your benefit and protection, so follow them closely.

◆ You will find a glossary of useful terms at the end of this guide. Refer to this glossary if you encounter unfamiliar terms.

◆ Always keep legal documents in a safe place and in a location known to your spouse, family, personal representative or attorney.

Table of contents

Introduction to Last Wills Made E-Z™

In ancient Egypt, the pharaohs didn't need wills; they simply loaded up their tombs with all their worldly goods, to be taken with them into the afterlife.

Fortunately, we've wised up a bit since then.

You can't take it with you—but you can be sure about what happens to it after you pass from this life into the next by creating the single most important document you will ever make: your last will and testament.

Unfortunately, most people either think they don't need one or that there's plenty of time to make one. The truth is everybody needs one, and the sooner you make it the better.

Fortunately, it's not that complicated (unless you're someone like Bill Gates or Prince Charles, then you might have some work ahead of you). All you really need is this guide, and to decide two things: who you want to take care of distributing your worldly goods, and who you want to receive them. The rest will fall into place.

Of course, making a will involves a little more than signing your name at the bottom, and you may, in the end, decide you need to use an attorney to complete it. Either way, the information in this guide will help clear the cobwebs off this legal topic and leave you with a last will—made E-Z!

Chapter 1

Everyone needs a will

What you'll find in this chapter:

➡ What a last will & testament is

➡ Why you need to make a will

➡ Who can make a will

➡ What an estate plan is

➡ Other documents you need

What is a will?

DEFINITION

In its simplest terms, a will is a formal and legally enforceable statement of how you wish to dispose of your property upon your death. The person(s) who inherit your property are your *beneficiaries*.

A valid will allows your last wishes to be protected by state law. Because it can be changed at any time prior to your death, your will can be used to express a variety of emotions: kindness, anger, surprise, appreciation, etc.

E-Z TIP

Wills may be used to stimulate others to act, to express compassion, to provide the means to decide, to get revenge, to surprise beneficiaries, and to show appreciation for hard work and loyalty.

A will is the simplest form of an estate plan. It is also the most important document of any estate plan, since it is the one item that makes clear what you want done with the things you leave behind.

Why is a will important?

Without a will you cannot control who will inherit your property upon your death. Should you die without a will, your property will be distributed according to the laws of your state. This "state will" may be totally inconsistent with your personal wishes. The law may demand that your property be given to distant relatives whom you have little or no feeling for, instead of to a good friend and neighbor of 20 years whom you would choose to inherit your property.

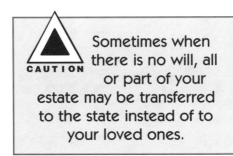

CAUTION Sometimes when there is no will, all or part of your estate may be transferred to the state instead of to your loved ones.

Even if you believe that you have nothing of value, a will can cover an unexpected inheritance, an accident claim or even a wrongful death award. With a valid will, you decide who your beneficiaries will be. These are the people *you* want to inherit your property.

note Your will may be used to forgive debts as well as to pay debts (including taxes) by designating what property is to be used to pay those debts.

A valid will enables you to name a guardian for your minor children. You can feel secure that you have guaranteed your children's education and upbringing. Your will also gives you the opportunity to select your *personal representative*. He or she is the person you choose to administer your estate.

DEFINITION

Who should make a will?

Every adult should have an up-to-date will. There are only two qualifications necessary to prepare a valid will:

1) **You must be of legal age.** The legal age in all states is 18, with these exceptions: in Alabama you must be 19 to bequeath real estate and 18 to bequeath personal property. In Georgia, you may be a minor older than 14 so long as you are also married and, therefore, considered emancipated. Iowa and New Hampshire also allow any married minor to make a will. Idaho allows any emancipated minor to make a will. Likewise, any member of the armed forces or maritime service is eligible in Indiana and Oregon.

2) **You must be of sound mind** when you prepare and sign the will. "Sound mind" simply means that you must understand what you are giving away and to whom you are giving it. You must also prepare

DEFINITION

your will free from implied or actual threats, pressure or trickery. Even evidence of mental illness or ongoing psychiatric care does not automatically prevent you from preparing a valid will. Simple absent-mindedness or forgetfulness is not evidence of mental illness. Should you have a

> *note*
> You must also prepare your will free of undue influence threats, pressure, trickery or other fraud. Most undue influence cases are filed against attorneys who are named as beneficiaries in a will they drafted for the suing client.

documented history of serious mental disorders, it may be wise to consult with a qualified medical practitioner just prior to preparing your will. This will help to establish your competency, which could be useful if the will should later be contested.

It is not necessary to be a citizen of the United States to make a will, but it is important to prepare your will in the state where you currently live. This makes the transfer of your personal property after your death much easier and smoother for your beneficiaries. If your will is valid in the state where it was drafted, it is valid in all other states.

note

> **note** In the course of making your will, and planning your estate, you must choose your domicile—your legal residence. If you live in more than two states, your legal residence is usually the state in which you pay taxes, register to vote, and have registered and titled your car.

Last will and estate planning

"Death and taxes are inevitable; at least death doesn't get worse every year..." The unknown author was right. Taxes and tax issues can become a serious concern for those who must settle an estate after a loved one passes. Without a will, you can't ensure that the property you leave behind goes to the people you want it to. In addition, without careful planning, your heirs may encounter some serious tax and property ownership issues. Therefore, it smart and considerate to have your estate in order today, before it is too late. A last will is the single most important thing you can do to prepare for this inevitable event. You may also take a few additional steps to help guarantee a more comfortable future for your loved ones, family and friends:

> **Definition:**
> *Estate.* An estate includes all the assets, including joint assets, and all the liabilities you leave at the time of your death.

• create a *Living Trust*. An excellent way to avoid the difficulties of probate, living trusts enable you to transfer your property directly to the trust of your beneficiaries during your life, without court involvement. After your death, the person you appoint to handle the trust may then simply transfer ownership to the beneficiaries you named in the trust.

• create a *Living Will & Power of Attorney for Healthcare.* These legal documents state your wishes about the type of medical treatment and life-prolonging procedures you would permit should disability leave you unable to speak on your own behalf. This helps ease the burden for your loved ones when striving to make important decisions on your behalf.

• organize and review your insurance and retirement benefits. Make certain your golden years are secure and your loved ones are cared for.

• seek tax advice to ensure your estate and loved ones are not overwhelmed with estate and death taxes (see appendix for financial resources).

When you begin planning for the future, even the simplest steps provide enormous peace-of-mind. E-Z Legal Forms, Inc. has the documents, the definitions, and the forms for your estate planning needs. The order form in the back of this guide provides more information to help you start today to plan for tomorrow.

Dying without a valid will

2

Chapter 2
Dying without a valid will

What you'll find in this chapter:

⇒ What dying "intestate" means

⇒ What happens when you have no will

⇒ The Laws of Intestate Succession

⇒ Beneficiaries and heirs

⇒ The three types of property

Unfortunately, people often delay preparing their wills. Some may dread the discussion of death. Some feel that their estates are not large enough to require a will. Some feel that they don't have the time to prepare a will.

Dying intestate

DEFINITION

When someone dies without having prepared a valid will, that person is said to have died "intestate."

note

Because he died without a will, the valuable estate of Pablo Picasso was one of the most complicated to settle of all time. It was finally settled at a cost of over 30 million. The estate of the 20th century's most famous artist included 1,885 paintings, 1,228 sculptures, 7,089 drawings, 30,000 prints, 150 sketchbooks, and 3,222 ceramic works as well as homes, gold, cash and bonds.

The laws that govern the distribution of property in such an estate are known as the Laws of Intestate Succession. These are state laws applied in exactly the same way to all estates that are not governed by wills. These laws determine who your beneficiaries, your administrator and the guardian of your children will be.

If you die intestate, your surviving spouse automatically inherits a certain percentage of your estate. That percentage differs from state to state, depending upon whom your other surviving relatives are. Any and all surviving parents, children, grandchildren or

> **Definition:** *Heir* vs. *beneficiary.* These words may be used interchangeably. To be technical, however, an heir is defined as a person legally due to inherit with or without a will (generally blood relations); but a beneficiary inherits through a will or other document, such as an insurance policy.

other descendants will affect how your estate's assets are divided. Again, you have absolutely no say in how your assets will be distributed if you leave no valid will.

For example, Bruce and Helen had a sizeable, jointly held estate, a home in Pennsylvania and no children together. Neither had found the time or realized the importance of preparing wills. Bruce died first, followed a few days later by Helen. The Pennsylvania laws of intestacy distributed all of the jointly held property to Helen's brother, whom Bruce hated. Unfortunately, Bruce's three children from a previous marriage received none of Bruce's jointly held assets.

> **Definition:** *Next of Kin* is not the same as the term *Heirs.* Next of kin refers exclusively to those who are related by blood while heirs usually refers to anyone who is entitled to inherit property from the deceased, under state law. Thus, a spouse is an heir but not next of kin.

Intestate succession

DEFINITION

Who inherits what if you have no will? The Laws of Intestate Succession, drafted by each state, determines who is to inherit. Intestate succession means the order of which heirs receive the estate of someone who has died without a will.

Many states have adopted the Civil Law method: Under this diagram (see below), each person's relationship to the decedent (the deceased) is assigned a numerical value or degree. Person's with the lowest number who are nearest the deceased are the first in line to inherit.

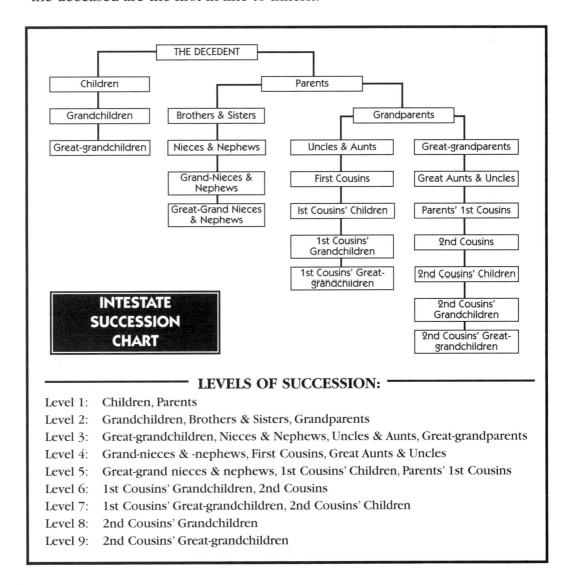

INTESTATE SUCCESSION CHART

─────────────── **LEVELS OF SUCCESSION:** ───────────────

Level 1:   Children, Parents

Level 2:   Grandchildren, Brothers & Sisters, Grandparents

Level 3:   Great-grandchildren, Nieces & Nephews, Uncles & Aunts, Great-grandparents

Level 4:   Grand-nieces & -nephews, First Cousins, Great Aunts & Uncles

Level 5:   Great-grand nieces & nephews, 1st Cousins' Children, Parents' 1st Cousins

Level 6:   1st Cousins' Grandchildren, 2nd Cousins

Level 7:   1st Cousins' Great-grandchildren, 2nd Cousins' Children

Level 8:   2nd Cousins' Grandchildren

Level 9:   2nd Cousins' Great-grandchildren

This product does not constitute the rendering of legal advice or services. This product is intended for informational use only and is not a substitute for legal advice. State laws vary, so consult an attorney on all legal matters. This product was not prepared by a person licensed to practice law in this state.

23

What happens to your property?

Personal property

The law of the state where the deceased lived determines how his or her personal property will be distributed if there is no valid will. One type of personal property is usually called tangible property, which is anything, other than real estate, that can be touched.

DEFINITION

Automobiles, computers, books, furniture, silverware, tools, coin and stamp collections, clothing and other personal effects are common examples of tangible property.

note

There are three different types of property: *Real* (real estate property and its buildings), *tangible* (property you can touch and use in its physical form), and also *intangible* (property that may be represented by paper such as stocks and bonds or copyrights and patents).

Definition:
Escheat. When there is no will, and there is no surviving spouse or identifiable kin, estate property is said to escheat, or pass to the state. In some states, real estates passes to the state in which it is located (even if the deceased did not live there) while personal property passes to the state where the deceased lived.

Intangible personal property consists of stocks, bonds, patents, copyrights, checks, drafts and notes. They are considered intangible because they represent your ownership of something else. For example, a check is intangible because it only represents your money, but it is not your money itself.

Real property

The law of the state where the real estate is located determines how your real property will be distributed if there is no will. Because state laws vary widely, it is possible for your real estate, located within your state, to be transferred differently from your real estate that is outside of your state. Without a valid will, the transfer of your real property may be subject to untimely delays and additional expenses.

Which will and why

3

Chapter 3
Which will and why

What you'll find in this chapter:

⮕ The holographic will

⮕ Which states accept which types of will

⮕ When you can make an oral will

⮕ Why joint wills are not a good idea

⮕ Last will vs. living will

DEFINITION

People have used many types of wills over the years. Today, however, many of them are no longer valid. In the process of *probate*, the procedure by which a will is determined to be valid, the courts found too many problems associated with oral wills and unwitnessed wills. In order to make it easier to prepare a valid will, the courts have established specific requirements. Today, pre-printed forms are available to help people avoid the pitfalls found in some of the wills described below.

The holographic will

DEFINITION

A holographic will is a handwritten, unwitnessed will. It must be written, dated and signed entirely in the handwriting of the *testator*, or person leaving the will.

Holographic wills are valid in the following states:

Alaska	North Dakota
Arizona	Oklahoma
California	Pennsylvania
Idaho	Puerto Rico
Kentucky	South Dakota
Louisiana	Texas
Maine	Utah
Michigan	Virginia
Mississippi	West Virginia
Montana	Wisconsin
Nevada	Wyoming

New York also recognizes holographic wills made by members of the armed forces (including merchant marines) during armed conflict.

Difficulties with holographic wills are common. Pre-printed wills, such as statutory wills (state-authorized will forms), and professionally prepared wills may contain certain standard provisions overlooked in informal wills such as the holographic will. Therefore, holographic wills could possibly encounter difficulty in probate. Any written but unwitnessed will is considered extremely unreliable and often does not stand up in court. Formal, pre-printed legal forms offer a far more reliable option that is increasingly adopted as the format to use.

The nuncupative will

A *nuncupative will* is an oral will, or unwritten will. Although this

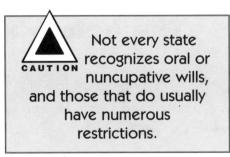

Not every state recognizes oral or nuncupative wills, and those that do usually have numerous restrictions.

type of will is usually made before witnesses, it is valid only when the testator is in immediate peril of dying (sometimes called a Last Sickness Will). Generally, you cannot leave property valued at more than $1,000 in a nuncupative will. Nuncupative wills made by soldiers and sailors in active service are recognized by many states.

The joint will

A *joint will* is the single will of two or more testators, such as a husband and wife. Because people may separate, lose their copy of the will or destroy the will without the other's knowledge or consent, it is always best to prepare a separate will for each testator. This should be done even if the wills are identical.

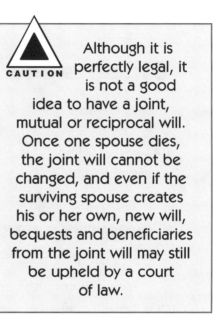

CAUTION Although it is perfectly legal, it is not a good idea to have a joint, mutual or reciprocal will. Once one spouse dies, the joint will cannot be changed, and even if the surviving spouse creates his or her own, new will, bequests and beneficiaries from the joint will may still be upheld by a court of law.

The mutual will

A *mutual will* is also called a *reciprocal will*. Here you find two identical but separate wills prepared by two different testators, each naming the other as beneficiary. Each contains an agreement that neither testator will make any changes in his or her will after the death of the other. Different states tend to define the terms "mutual" and "reciprocal" differently. Some states call these "joint wills."

To avoid confusion, it is best to define all of the terms and conditions of your will as clearly as possible. Simply make two completely separate wills that are not identical, yet name each other as beneficiaries.

The conditional will

A conditional will depends upon a specific event or situation occurring. If that event does not occur, then the will is void. For example, a person who wants his will to be effective only if he dies a natural death would use a conditional will.

Videotaped or audiotaped wills

No state recognizes these as valid wills. However, videotaping is one method of establishing the identity and alertness of the testator. If you want to use videotape, accompany it with a formal written will.

Computer wills

You can create your will on a computer yourself or using software for that purpose, but be sure to print it out and sign it before witnesses. An unsigned and unwitnessed will stored on your computer is not a valid will. It must be printed out and properly signed and witnessed to be recognized by the court as a valid will.

The living will

This guide deals only with testamentary wills, those that dispose of your property after death. A living will, in contrast, indicates at what point you wish to terminate medical attempts to prolong your life. For more information on living wills, see E-Z Legal's guide *Living Wills Made E-Z*.

Your Last Will & Testament

4

Chapter 4

Your Last Will & Testament

What you'll find in this chapter:
➠ The parts of a will
➠ Your personal representative
➠ Bequests
➠ Witnesses
➠ Signing your will

Elements of a valid will

There are three elements that the court looks for when it determines if a will is valid:

1) The will must be in writing. Although some states recognize an oral will, they do so under very limited conditions. An oral will that is made on a death bed or by soldiers in the military are examples of such conditions. Every state recognizes a written will.

2) The will must be signed by the testator. The testator can direct another to sign for him providing that the person signs the will in the testator's presence. You do not have to know how to write your name in order to sign your will, because the law will accept any

mark that you want to use as your signature. Most state laws require that the testator sign at the end of the will.

3)   The will must be attested to. This simply means that there must be at least two or three adult witnesses, who will not benefit from your estate, who are willing to sign your will. These witnesses must be of sound mind and must sign in the presence of the testator, a notary, and each other. They must also include their addresses. Remember, none of the beneficiaries of your will can be witnesses. Be absolutely sure that your witnesses will receive no inheritance from your will and that they are not your personal representative, an appointed guardian, your spouse, or any other relative. Your witnesses must be of legal age and understand what it is they are signing, and they must live locally in case a question should arise concerning the validity of the will. Don't forget that the will must also be notarized. This establishes the fact that you and your witnesses did sign the will, so that there can be no question about the identity of the persons who signed the will.

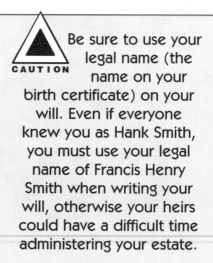

Be sure to use your legal name (the name on your birth certificate) on your will. Even if everyone knew you as Hank Smith, you must use your legal name of Francis Henry Smith when writing your will, otherwise your heirs could have a difficult time administering your estate.

A look at your will

Examine the Last Will & Testament form in the back of this guide. It contains the following elements:

I. The Opening Clause

The opening paragraph generally begins with the words "BE IT KNOWN." The purpose of this paragraph is to identify you as the person making the will, to identify your permanent address, to declare that you were of sound mind when the will was made, to declare this document to be your last will and testament, and to revoke and cancel any prior wills you might have made.

II. The Personal Representative Clause

The personal representative paragraph follows, beginning with the words "PERSONAL REPRESENTATIVE." This is where you name the personal representative that you choose to administer or manage your estate after your death. Be sure to fill out the name of the alternate that you have chosen as well.

In this paragraph you are instructing the personal representative to pay any debts that you legally owe and your funeral expenses out of the money in your estate. You are also instructing the court that it is not necessary for your personal representative to post a bond. Furthermore, you state that you want no experts to be called in to estimate the value of your estate unless this practice is required by law. The cost of such an appraisal will be deducted from the value of the estate. Additionally, a conflict can arise regarding the appraisal and the testator's estimated value.

III. The Guardian Clause

Next is the guardian clause, beginning with the word "GUARDIAN." In this clause you name a guardian for your minor children. The guardian's role is to take care of your minor children in the event that neither of the natural parents are living. Some of the duties of the guardian are:

a) to possess and manage the minor's property

b) to manage and invest the minor's assets

c) to use the funds for the benefit of the minor

d) to provide regular accounts to the probate court

e) to file and pay the minor's taxes

f) to distribute the remaining funds to the minor when he or she reaches adulthood

You would usually appoint your spouse as guardian, but in the event that your spouse dies before you do or you both die at the same time, you need to appoint an alternate. It may not be a good idea to choose the child's grandparents if they are advanced in age. Since you want someone who can offer the best care for your child, a close relative who is willing to accept the responsibility is a good choice.

In addition to being responsible for providing care, comfort and education for the child, the guardian is also responsible for the child's property. Therefore, if you are leaving property to a minor, that property must be entrusted to the guardian. While you are considering the finances that will be necessary to support the child, if it is within your means to do so, consider compensating the guardian. The guardian, like the personal representative, is going to be asked to post a bond with the court. While this bond is an expression of good faith, you may state in your will that the guardian is to serve without having to post the bond.

IV. The Bequests

Here is the main body of the will, beginning with the word "BEQUESTS." (Sometimes, the term "legacies" or "devises" is used instead of the word "bequests"). This is the part of the will in which you leave the gifts to your beneficiaries. You name the specific person and the specific item that you are leaving that person. This is known as the *dispositive clause* in the will,

DEFINITION

> **note** You can request another person sign for you (in your and the witness' presence), if you are physically unable to do so yourself. Your will must then state that another person is signing for you.

because it is the place for you to dispose of your property.

This guide provides extra pages for you to make your bequests. Use as many as are necessary to leave all of your gifts, and make copies if more pages are needed.

Be sure to sign the bottom of each page. Notice that there is also a space for you to number each page. By filling in the page number at the bottom of each page and indicating the total number of pages in your will, you are preventing anyone from adding or deleting unauthorized pages.

V. The Signature Clause

Beginning with the words "IN WITNESS WHEREOF," this clause introduces the testator's signature. The testator's signature establishes the end of the will and the date on which it was signed or completed. When signing this will, the testator must use exactly the same name that he or she used in the opening paragraph.

> **Definition:**
> *Signature.* An "X" marks the spot! A signature is defined as any mark the person making the will intends to be his or her signature.

VI. The Witness Clause

The witness clause, beginning with the word "WITNESSED," comes after the testator's signature but before the witnesses' signatures. In this clause, the witnesses are simply stating that on this date the testator and witnesses signed the will in each other's presence and in the presence of the notary public.

Make certain your witnesses actually see you sign your will. Harvey, his witnesses, and the notary were gathered in Harvey's living room to sign his will. However, Harvey had failing eyesight and withdrew to the brightly lit kitchen to sign his will. Because neither the notary nor the witnesses actually saw Harvey's hand sign the will, the court declared the will to be invalid.

Just how many witnesses do you need? All but two states now require two witness signatures on a will (any extra witnesses have no legal effect in those states). Like the testator, the witnesses must be at least 18 years of age and of sound mind.

It is important that the witnesses not only sign their names but provide their current addresses in case they have to be contacted. You will find that three signature lines are provided. Be sure to have at least two impartial witnesses sign your will (three in Vermont and Louisiana).

VII. The Acknowledgment Clause

In the acknowledgment clause, the testator and witnesses sign their names in each other's presence and in the presence of the notary public. This is known also known as the "self-proving clause."

The acknowledgment clause acts as an affidavit, so that when a will is signed and notarized, the witnesses do not have to appear in court. All states but Maryland, Ohio, Vermont, and the District of Columbia recognize this option or use an affidavit that is not part of the will itself. In those states, the personal representative must prove the will in court.

It's a good idea to sign mportant documents like wills in blue ink rather than black ink. That way you'll know if the will is the original document or a photocopy.

VIII. The Notary Clause

The notary clause begins with the words "State of." In the last paragraph of the will, the notary public is swearing to the signatures on the will, and is guaranteeing that the will was signed in his or her presence. In some states, the notary's guarantee allows the will to be admitted into probate without needing the affidavits or appearances of any of the witnesses. In all states, having your will notarized eliminates any question about who signed it.

Preparing your Last Will & Testament

When you are ready to begin filling out your will, follow these step-by-step instructions. If you make a copy of the will form, you can use it as a worksheet.

CAUTION Do not make any changes directly onto a will after it has been completed, signed and witnessed, because those changes will not be valid. Prepare a codicil to the will, or better yet, make a new will.

1) Type your name (or print in ink), so the will is identified as yours.

2) Restate your name.

3) State the city or town where you reside. It is not necessary to use your street address.

4) State the county and state where you reside. This is where your will shall be probated.

5) Identify whom you wish as your personal representative.

6) State the address of your personal representative.

7) State your choice of alternate personal representative should your first-named personal representative be unable or unwilling to serve.

8) State the address of the alternate personal representative.

9) Identify who you wish as the guardian of any minor children.

10) State the name of the alternate guardian.

11) List your special bequests. Note that the sample will contains only two special bequests, but you may have many such bequests. Use copies of the enclosed blank will page if you need additional pages.

12) After you have listed your special bequests, specify whom should inherit the balance of your property using the residuary clause. Name contingent beneficiaries in the event your primary beneficiary should predecease you.

13) Number each page. Examples: "page one of two," "page three of eight."

14) Initial each page of your will

15) State the day of the month the will was signed.

16) State the month and year.

17) Sign your will exactly as your name first appears.

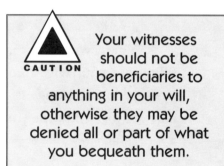

Your witnesses should not be beneficiaries to anything in your will, otherwise they may be denied all or part of what you bequeath them.

18) State the date.

19) Acknowledge that the document is your will in front of the witnesses.

20) Each witness should sign his or her full name and also provide a complete address. Make certain your witnesses are disinterested parties.

21) Print or type the names of the testator and witnesses again, followed by their signatures.

22) The acknowledgement is normally completed by the notary. The notary should be present at the signing, along with the witnesses. Be certain your notary and witnesses see you sign and see each other sign.

Your personal representa-tive

Chapter 5

Your personal representative

What you'll find in this chapter:
➠ The role of the personal representative
➠ Administrators and executors
➠ Duties of the personal representative
➠ Gift and estate taxes
➠ Your personal inventory

Your will must name a personal representative and authorize him or her to probate your estate. This person makes the important administrative decisions, gathers the assets, and distributes them to the beneficiaries after your death. The personal representative is sometimes called the "executor" or "administrator" if a male, and "executrix" or "administratrix" if a female.

By taking the time to prepare your will, you have the advantage of naming your personal representative.

Definition: The terms *executor* and *administrator* are often used interchangeably; in this guide we use the term "personal representative" to avoid this confusion. Technically, an *executor* is the person the testator chooses to handle the affairs of their estate. An *administrator* is a person appointed by the probate court to assume the duties of an executor should a person die without a will.

Failure to name a personal representative does not invalidate your will. However, the court will try to find a relative who is willing to administer your estate. This can be a time-consuming and fruitless process, often resulting in the court finally appointing a total stranger to administer your affairs. If you leave no will at all, the court again appoints a stranger to take charge of your affairs. This stranger, completely unaware of and unbounded by your last wishes, distributes your property according to state law.

What makes a good personal representative?

Since the primary duty of your personal representative is to carry out the terms of your will, he or she must be someone responsible. You are trusting this person to act in the best interest of your estate. A spouse or close friend is often a good choice for this job. The duties are not difficult, but an attorney will probably be hired by your personal representative to process the probate forms.

Do not choose a minor, a convicted felon or someone unwilling to serve. Eliminate anyone who might have a conflict of interest. The court will pay close attention to this point. For example, do not choose your business partner if he or she will have to evaluate the assets of your share of the business. It is also important that your personal representative live in the same state that you live in. Sometimes a bank representative is named personal representative for an estate, but fees for this service tend to be high. Inquire at your bank if your are interested in naming your bank your personal representative.

Sometimes a testator names two people as his or her personal representatives, usually to avoid offending someone. Not only does this create much more paperwork, but it can create an awkward situation when the two personal representatives are unable to agree on an issue. Even at the risk of offending someone, it is far better to name only one personal representative to administer your estate.

In order to serve, your personal representative may be required by law to post a bond. This money is simply a way of assuring the state that the person you named will act in good faith. If you have sufficient trust and confidence in your choice, you may insert a clause in your will stating that your personal representative is to serve without posting a bond. Such a clause has been written into the Last Will & Testament in this guide. It reads:

"I further provide my personal representative shall not be required to post surety bond in this or any jurisdiction, and direct that no expert appraisal be made of my estate unless required by law."

A personal representative is paid a taxable commission or fee for his services. The fee is set either by state law or the court, and can range from one to six percent of the value of the estate. The larger the estate, the higher the fee. The fee may be waived, and often is, by the personal representative. This is accomplished by inserting a clause into your will that might read:

"I direct my personal representative to serve without compensation beyond the normal expenses associated with the administration of my estate."

Duties of the personal representative

To help you choose your personal representative and, perhaps, to make it easier for that person to serve, the following lists some of the typical duties and responsibilities of the position:

1) keep assets in the estate

2) receive assets from others

3) perform or refuse to perform the decedent's contracts

4) fulfill charitable pledges made by the decedent

5) deposit or invest the estate's assets in appropriate investments

6) acquire, abandon or sell assets of the estate

7) make repairs, erect or demolish buildings

8) subdivide, develop or improve land

9) lease from or to others with an option to purchase

10) enter into a mineral lease or similar agreement

11) vote securities in person or by proxy

12) insure assets against damage, loss and liability

13) insure himself or herself against liability to others

14) borrow money for the estate, with or without security, to be repaid from the estate's assets

15) advance money to protect the estate

16) arrange compromises with any person to whom the estate owes money

17) pay taxes, assessments and other expenses

18) sell stock rights

19) employ people

20) consent to the reorganization, merger or liquidation of a business

21) sell, mortgage or lease property in the estate

22) go to court to protect the estate from the claims of others

23) continue as an unincorporated business

24) incorporate any business

25) distribute the assets of the estate

Paying estate taxes

Many estates do not have to pay federal estate taxes, because there is a $600,000 exemption and an unlimited marital deduction. If the value of your estate is more than $600,000, or if it will be complex to administer, you should consult with a qualified estate planner or an attorney. Either will be able to offer you planning methods and strategies that may lower your tax liabilities.

Your estate may still be liable for paying federal and state income and gift taxes and state inheritance taxes. Note that all taxes must be paid from your estate before any bequests are distributed to your beneficiaries.

Your personal inventory

For your personal representative to administer your estate properly, at the time of your death he or she must have all the important information concerning your estate. This includes:

- A complete list of all of your assets. Include all of your real estate, the names of any co-owners and the location of any deeds. List all of your personal property and remember to write the replacement cost of each item—that is, what it would cost to replace the item in today's economy, not the price you originally paid for it.

- Copies of all group and individual insurance policies.

- Your vital records. Include your birth certificate, last will, marriage licenses and divorce decrees.

- Your cemetery plot deed and burial instructions or requests.

- All retirement, pension or employee benefit plans with specific death benefits, including military records.

- An inventory of all legal documents concerning your assets and liabilities, including any business agreements, partnerships, stockholder agreements, trust agreements or wills under which you are a beneficiary, pre-nuptial agreements, spouse's will, bonds, stocks, bank accounts, mortgages and any valuable special collections that you may have.

- Your tax returns for the past three years, including any gift tax returns.

- A complete list of all of your debts and obligations, including any pledged assets, mortgages, personal notes or margin accounts with stockbrokers.

- Any other records that would help establish the value of your estate or that would help in the transfer of property after your death, including those provided in the Last Will & Testament in this guide.

Keep all of this information together in an envelope clearly marked "will." Make copies, and store one set with each copy of your will. You can ensure your privacy by distributing a copy of the Document Locator form to your personal representative or attorney, rather than providing all your personal records. This will enable him or her to collect the information needed to administer your estate after your death. As your circumstances change, review and revise this information, as well as your will, regularly. Replace out-of-date copies with current ones and alert anyone having copies to the changes you have made.

Making your bequests

6

Chapter 6

Making your bequests

What you'll find in this chapter:

⮞ How to make a bequest

⮞ Leaving property in your will

⮞ Leaving money in your will

⮞ Types of beneficiaries

⮞ Forgiving debts

How to say what you really mean

Preparing your own will is not difficult. However, you must pay particular attention to the language you use to make your bequests. If you state in your will, "I leave my watch to my daughter," you know which watch and which daughter you are referring to. Would this be clear to someone else? You may have the diamond-studded Rolex in mind for your bequest, but you have forgotten about the broken Timex you threw into your desk drawer two years ago when the battery ran down. To avoid any confusion, describe the exact watch and the exact daughter that you are referring to.

The language you use in your will establishes your intentions. The more specific the language, the clearer your language will be to others.

Be as precise as possible

Do not use words such as: *desire, hope, want, pray, would like, believe* or *request* when making your bequests. These are not words of intent; they simply reflect your wishes. Use as much detail when describing your property as is necessary to identify it.

Here is another example of a bequest that is too vague. "I give my collection of books to my sister Alice Smith." Unless you want your sister to inherit every single book in your home, you have to be more specific. A clearer statement of your intentions may be, "I give my collection of 50 rare, leatherbound first editions located in the oak bookcase under the window in my study to my sister Alice Smith." In this case, your sister would only inherit 50 valuable volumes.

When describing real property, list the addresses, plot, parcel, lot number and the name of the development. Addresses, streets, and even communities occasionally change their names.

Be careful when using words that indicate quantity. Words such as *all, every* and *entire* mean that there are **no** exceptions. In addition, words such as *some, few,* and *several* have no precise meaning other than to indicate that you mean more than one. Try to describe the number of items whenever possible. When you mention your children, name each child that you are bequeathing property to. Do not use phrases such as "my children" unless you mean all of your children, including natural children, stepchildren and nonmarital children. Never describe your beneficiaries in general terms.

> **note**
> Under modern state law, an adopted child named in a will is treated as if the adopted parent is the natural parent of that child.

Since many charities and organizations have similar names, the beneficiary of a charitable bequest must be specifically identified. "I give $2,000 to the Cancer Foundation" is an unclear bequest. Properly phrased, it might read: "I give $2,000 to the American Cancer Society located at 2937 N.W. 8 St., Miami, Florida 22345." This charity is properly identified because the reader knows which cancer society you mean and exactly where it is located. You may also designate that you want your bequest to go to a special fund within the charity. Monetary bequests are often left to library funds, research funds, building funds, and educational funds.

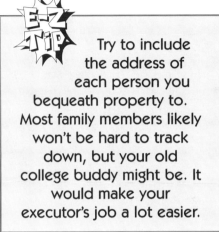

E-Z TIP

Try to include the address of each person you bequeath property to. Most family members likely won't be hard to track down, but your old college buddy might be. It would make your executor's job a lot easier.

Making specific bequests

With special bequests, you leave specific assets to certain beneficiaries. Bequests should always be clear, complete and specific regarding who is to receive which property. For example:

"I give my 1987 Chevrolet Caprice to my son Harry Smith."

or

"I bequeath to the Second Baptist Church of Center City the sum of $10,000 to be used in any manner the church deems proper."

Your bequest may be personal property or real estate; you may name an individual or an institution as your beneficiary. The gift does not need to have any monetary importance. It may have personal meaning instead. For example, you might leave a personal souvenir to a friend to remind him of a time shared together, or an admired book to a colleague, or some jewelry to a daughter. These are the types of gifts that require careful thought.

Due to mergers and acquisitions, the ownership of public companies can change in a heartbeat. If bequeathing this type of property, it is best to add a phrase such as: "I bequeath to John Doe my stock in XYZ, Inc. or equivalent stock in their corporate successor at the time of my death."

Your specific bequest must also indicate whether the property you are gifting is being given free and clear, that is, without any debts or claims against it. If there is a debt attached to the gift, you must indicate whether the debt is to be paid from your general estate or by the beneficiary. of that gift.

You must be as clear as possible regarding the distribution of these gifts. Here are some examples:

"I leave to my daughter Mary Smith my home at 5 Maple Street, Center City, subject to all mortgages."

or

"I leave my dear friend Harry Carlson my 1994 Chris Craft Sedan Cruiser, free of all encumbrances."

It is very important when making your list of bequests that you include the list in your will. Do not attach a separate list to your will, because the courts may not consider that list part of your actual will. Most courts will not accept attachments to wills.

Contingent beneficiaries

It is possible that one of the beneficiaries you name in your will may die before you do. Just as it is always wise to name an alternate personal representative and alternate guardian for your minor children, it is wise to name an alternate for each beneficiary that you list in your will. You might use a clause such as:

"I give my 1995 Honda Accord to Jack Smith, or if he fails to survive me, I give that property to his daughter, Michelle Smith."

Theoretically, there is no limit to how many levels of alternate beneficiaries you may name. Alternate beneficiaries may be effectively used to create different plans for distributing your estate. You may for example, feel obligated to leave everything to a specific person but in the event that person predeceases you, you may then feel free to make specific bequests to other relatives, close friends, or even to charities.

> **note** You cannot use a will to change the beneficiaries of your life insurance policy. The policy itself must be changed and the appropriate insurance company notified.

Remember, if you name an alternate beneficiary for a child or other dependent, that alternate does not have to be another child or dependent. Be sure to specify the share each of your beneficiaries is to receive.

> **note** Antilapse statutes provide that, should a beneficiary of your property die before you, and you haven't rewritten your will, the property will go to their next heir in line rather than revert back to your estate. Without anti-lapse laws, all the property you had intended to leave that beneficiary could go back to the bulk of the estate and not end up in an actual family member's hands.

If you leave property to your children but a child dies before you do, should the deceased child's share be distributed among your other children? Would you prefer the share to be distributed among your child's children (your grandchildren)?

There is no correct answer to this, but here two alternative ways of expressing your wishes: the per capita bequest and the per stirpes request.

Per capita bequest

A per capita bequest leaves property distributed in equal shares to all entitled beneficiaries, as in this example:

"I leave all my property to my children who may survive me, in equal shares."

The key to this wording is the fact that each child receives an equal share. Simply divide the property by the number of children surviving you.

Caution: Al bequeathed $100,000 to his daughter in bonds and $100,000 to his son in cash. However, the value of the bonds had dropped to $50,000 at the time of Al's death. He should have left each child 50 percent of his estate if he wanted each to have an equal amount of money.

Per stirpes bequest

A per stirpes bequest divides property up in a more specific manner, such as:

"I leave all my property in equal shares to my children, but if any child shall predecease me, I leave that child's share to his or her children equally."

Here the grandchild or grandchildren can inherit only the proportion or amount that their parent was entitled to inherit. The children take the place of the parent and stand in his or her shoes for the purpose of inheritance. This is often called *inheritance by rights of representation.*

It is wiser to choose a per capita bequest over a per stirpes bequest. For example, Sally bequeathed all of her property equally to her two sons, Charles and Harry, or their lineal descendants, per stirpes. Charles had one child and Harry had two children. Both Charles and Harry died before Sally. When Sally dies, Charles' child inherits one half of the estate while Harry's children must share their half. Therefore, Harry's children each receive one quarter of the estate. If Sally had left her estate per capita instead of per stirpes, each grandchild would have received one third of the estate.

Other contingent bequests

CAUTION

Do not name your pet as a beneficiary. Animals are considered property, and one property cannot own another property. If you have strong feelings about providing for the future care of your pet, feel free to make outside arrangements, perhaps with a veterinarian. If you intend to leave your pet to a beneficiary as a gift, do not surprise that person with the pet. Get his or her permission first.

Do not include a body or organ bequest in your will. It is unlikely that your will can be read in time to allow for the donation. You should make separate arrangements for this type of donation. Even if you can make the donation, remember that medical schools do not accept every donated body, so be sure to make alternative arrangements in case yours is rejected.

Residuary bequests

DEFINITION

Another type of bequest you should make in your will is the residuary bequest. The "residuary" clause names the "residuary beneficiary"—the person or organization who will receive (other than specific bequests) the remainder of your estate. Because the residuary clause distributes your remaining property, it is often called your "safety net." It accounts for assets that might fall through the cracks in your will. Suppose you forgot to include a valuable piece of jewelry in your bequests, or you received a valuable painting after you prepared your will. What would happen to those assets when your property was distributed? If you have no residuary clause in your will, overlooked assets would be distributed as though you had no will.

With a residuary clause, you designate exactly who should receive any overlooked assets. In this situation, when you have made other bequests, your residuary clause might read:

"I leave all the rest of my property to my wife, Hilda Jones."

Of course, you do not have to make any specific bequests in your will. In this case, your will would contain only a single residuary bequest. This type of residuary clause might read:

"I leave all my property to my wife Hilda Jones."

Although no particular language is necessary, a more complete residuary clause might read:

"I leave all the rest, residue, and remainder of my estate, real, personal, and mixed, of whatever kind and wherever situated, in which I may have any interest or to which I may be entitled or over which I may have power of appointment, to my wife Hilda Jones."

Another function of the Residuary Clause is to act as a "safety net." Since it distributes any portion of your estate not accounted for by specific bequests, anything you have forgotten to include will be accounted for under your will. That valuable piece of jewelry or valuable painting you acquired long after you had prepared your will could fall through the cracks in your will; the Residuary Clause prevents this from happening.

Forgiving debts

A will may be used to cancel a debt that one of your beneficiaries owes you. There are three ways to do this.

1) You may use your will to legally release the person from his or her obligation to repay you, whether or not the person is left property. Simply state in the bequest section of your will something that might read like this:

"I formally release John Smith from his obligation to repay any outstanding balance remaining on the $10,000 that I loaned him on May 1, 1994."

2) Although John Smith owes you money, you may still want to leave him a bequest. If you want him to receive his full share of the bequest, insert a clause that might read like this:

"I bequeath $20,000 to John Smith and release him from his obligation to repay any money that he owes me. He is to receive the full amount of his bequest."

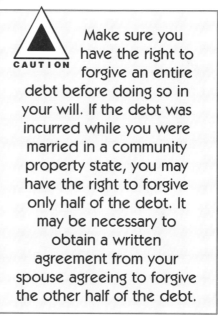

Make sure you have the right to forgive an entire debt before doing so in your will. If the debt was incurred while you were married in a community property state, you may have the right to forgive only half of the debt. It may be necessary to obtain a written agreement from your spouse agreeing to forgive the other half of the debt.

3) John Smith owes you money and you want your estate to be repaid. To accomplish this, make the bequest and deduct the outstanding debt from it. For example:

"I leave $10,000 to John Smith, less such balance on the $5,000 debt he owes me."

If John Smith still owed you $3,000, he would receive only $7,000 from your $10,000 bequest. What would happen to the remaining $3,000 that is still in your estate? It would be covered by the residuary clause, and would be inherited by the beneficiary of that clause.

A gift or a loan?

If you give $5,000 to your son during your lifetime, is it a gift or a loan? Your will needs to be clear and precise on these matters, since your son is probably a beneficiary in your will.

Clarify issues such as these now to avoid confusion when it's time to administer your estate.

Clause and effect

7

Chapter 7
Clause and effect

What you'll find in this chapter:

⇒ Writing clauses for adopted children

⇒ Writing clauses for simultaneous death

⇒ Writing clauses for funeral expenses

⇒ The pour-over clause

⇒ The credit shelter trust

The last will provided in this guide may cover all your needs. However, there are additional clauses that many people choose to include. If you feel any of the following clauses are appropriate to your situation, feel free to include them in your will. If you find it necessary to refer to a document outside of your will, or even to include that document itself in your will, be sure to use the *incorporation by reference* clause. There is no limit to the number of clauses you may add to your will, depending on your needs.

Adopted children clause

Most states treat adopted children as though they were the parents' natural children. However, different states use different words to describe children: "issues," "heirs," "descendants" or "children." If you include a clause in your will that clearly defines what you want the word "children" to mean, the possibility of any confusion can be avoided later on. Such a clause might read:

"By the use of the word 'child' or 'children' in this will, I mean any and all children lawfully adopted by me at any time before or after the making of this will."

Simultaneous death clause

A common question that you and your spouse might ask is, "What will happen to our will if we die together?" Simultaneous death affects the distribution of property. Every state has a plan for the distribution of your property in the event that you both

 CAUTION Stepchildren, unless legally adopted by the non-biological parent, only have rights to their biological parent's estate under intestate law. Likewise, children born out of wedlock can only inherit from a biological parent. A child born through artificial insemination inherits from the husband of the birth mother, not from the semen donor, and a child born from a surrogate mother has no rights to the estate of the surrogate mother but does have rights to his/her legal parents' estate.

die in a common disaster. Unfortunately, this state plan may be (and often is) counter to your wishes. A simultaneous death clause solves his problem. Without such a clause in your will, the state presumes that you, the testator, died first; the property is transferred to your deceased spouse and then immediately to your spouse's beneficiaries, not yours.

For example, Mary and John have separate wills. In John's will, John leaves most of his property to Mary and in Mary's will, Mary leaves most of her property to John. If Mary dies before John, John wants his property to go to his son from a previous marriage. Mary wants her property to go to her brother if John dies before she does. But according to state law, if John and Mary die simultaneously, John's property goes to Mary's brother and Mary's property goes to John's son. This is counter to the instructions in the wills.

A simultaneous death clause states that for the purpose of distributing property to those named in a will, the law should presume that the testator survives the beneficiary; that Mary died before John when his will is administered and that John died before Mary when her will is administered. In effect, this restores the original intentions of the will and allows the last wishes of each spouse to be honored.

It is always recommended, and in this case necessary, that each spouse have a separate will. Separate wills permit each estate to be administered separately. A sample simultaneous death clause might read:

"If my spouse and I should die under circumstances as would render it doubtful whether my spouse or I died first, then it shall be conclusively presumed for the purposes of this will that my spouse predeceased me."

You may also have a similar clause concerning simultaneous death with a beneficiary under your will. Such a clause might read:

"If any beneficiary and I should die under circumstances as would render it doubtful whether the beneficiary or I died first, then it shall be conclusively presumed for the purposes of my will that said beneficiary predeceased me."

No contest clause

Some states allow you to add a clause to your will that revokes any bequest to any beneficiary who challenges the will. This clause warns the challenger that if he or she loses the challenge, he or she receives nothing at all from the will. It is a good idea for you to leave a little more than the bare minimum to those people whom you wish to disinherit. By doing this and including a no contest clause, you encourage these potential challengers, such as disappointed relatives, to accept the terms of the will.

For example, if you had a no contest clause, Uncle Charlie may decide that keeping the $300 you left him is better than gambling on losing it if he tries to collect the $1,000 he feels he is entitled to.

A typical no contest clause might read:

"If my beneficiary under this will either directly or indirectly challenges the validity of this will, any bequest left to said beneficiary shall be revoked."

Cemetery bequest clause

While you may direct that all funeral expenses be paid from your estate, it is not a good idea to include specific funeral arrangements in your will, because the funeral may be over before the will is found. However, it is not uncommon to make a special bequest to a cemetery for the perpetual care of a cemetery plot.

These arrangements—in fact, all funeral arrangements—should be made in advance so that you can bequeath the appropriate amount of money.

A sample clause may read:

"I bequeath $5,000 to Mary Knoll Cemetery for the perpetual care of my cemetery plot."

Funeral expense clause

It is usually the responsibility of the personal representative to see that funeral expenses are paid out of the money in the estate, but some states make the surviving spouse responsible for those expenses. It is a good idea to include a clause directing where the money to pay the funeral expenses is to come from. A sample clause may read:

"My debts and expenses of my funeral and burial shall be paid out of my estate."

Incorporation by reference clause

To incorporate a separate document into your will, you must make reference to it in your will with this clause. A sample clause may read:

"I hereby intend to, and do, incorporate by reference into this will the following document dated January 1, 1998, which is now in existence at the time of this writing and is located at 500 Main Street, Anytown, PA. The document is described as follows: A listing of individual paintings and the intended beneficiary of each painting."

You may only incorporate a document into a will by reference if that document actually exists at the time the will is executed. Documents cannot be incorporated into the will as they come into existence, if at all, at some future time.

Pour-over clause

Even people who choose to avoid the time and cost of probate by putting all their assets in a living trust should have a will, if for no other reason than to insert a pour-over clause into it. A pour-over clause states that any asset inadvertently left out of a trust should, at the time of death, be automatically added to that trust.

For example, John Smith purchases a valuable coin for his collection and plans to do the paperwork necessary to transfer it to his living trust. But he is killed in an auto accident before he can do so. Can the coin still be placed in the living trust? Yes, through the use of a pour-over clause in John's will. This clause states that items outside of the living trust "pour over," or are automatically added to the trust upon the testator's death. A sample pour-over clause in John's will might read:

"The remainder of my estate, wherever located, I bequeath to the trustee or trustees named under a certain revocable living trust executed by me on January 1, 1995, between myself and the trustee of the John Smith Trust in the county of Anycounty and the state of Anystate, to be added to the principal of the trust and to be administered in all respects as an integral part of that trust."

The credit shelter trust

If you are married and your gross estate (including living trust property) exceeds the exemption amount in the chart below, you should consult an attorney or tax specialist.

The Economic Recovery Act of 1981 set the Unified Tax Credit Exemption at $600,000 for individuals, or $1,200,000 for couples, as the amount exempt from estate taxes. As of January 1, 1998, this amount began a graduated increase over the next eight years until a maximum of $1,000,000 per individual ($2,000,000 per couple) is reached. The increase occurs as follows:

UNIFIED TAX CREDIT EXEMPTIONS		
Year	Single	Couple
pre-1998	$600,000	$1,200,000
1998	$625,000	$1,250,000
1999	$650,000	$1,300,000
2000	$675,000	$1,350,000
2001	$675,000	$1,350,000
2002	$700,000	$1,400,000
2003	$700,000	$1,400,000
2004	$850,000	$1,700,000
2005	$950,000	$1,900,000
2006	$1,000,000	$2,000,000

In the event your gross estate as grantor exceeds the exemption amount in the chart above, you may minimize your estate taxes by having you and your spouse set up separate reciprocal living trusts often called "credit shelter trusts" or "A-B trusts." This estate planning tool allows your estate to pass to the trust rather than directly to the surviving spouse. The trust, in turn, provides the surviving spouse with a lifetime income from the trust. Since your trustee must be aware of your intention to use this type of trust, you may provide the following sample instructions:

"If my spouse shall survive me, I direct that my entire trust estate be given to my trustee(s) to be divided into two separate trusts which are herein referred to as 'Trust A' and 'Trust B.'

1) Trust A shall have placed into it the sum of $_____. Said sum represents one-half of the value of my adjusted gross estate as defined by the Internal Revenue Code for the purposes of the marital deduction. Trust A shall be reduced to the extent allowed under the Internal Revenue Codes, by the value of all assets that pass or have passed to my spouse other than by the terms of this paragraph and that satisfy the marital deduction.

2) Trust B shall have placed into it an amount equal to the balance of my residuary estate after deducting the amount allocated to Trust A."

Savings clause

In the event that any of the clauses in your will are found to be invalid, you do not want the entire will to be revoked. A savings clause accomplishes exactly that: it saves the will. A sample savings clause might read:

"In case any of the separate provisions in this will are found to be invalid, the invalidity of such a provision shall not affect the validity of any other provisions in this will, since it is my intention that each of the separate provisions shall be independent of each other, allowing all valid provisions to be enforced regardless of the validity of any of the others."

What cannot be done in a will

8

Chapter 8

What cannot be done in a will

What you'll find in this chapter:
⮕ Staying within the law
⮕ Different types of property
⮕ Life insurance policies
⮕ Disinheriting a spouse
⮕ Disinheriting children

Although there are very few restrictions on what you may say in a will, all states have imposed some limitations upon what a will may be used for, what you may give away, and how spouses and children are to be treated.

Is it lawful?

One of the basic principles that govern all wills is the idea of lawfulness. If it was illegal during your lifetime, you cannot use your will to make it legal.

- You cannot use your will to libel or defame another person. If you write a false statement about another person and it becomes a matter of public record, as a will does, your estate may be liable for damages. Do not try to damage another person's reputation through your will.

- You cannot require someone to commit an act that is illegal in order for that person to inherit under your will. A will cannot be used to violate public policy or command something be done that is not in the person's best interests; in some states, this includes requiring or forbidding a beneficiary to marry, work, or have children.

Definition:
Slayer Statutes are state statutes that prohibit anyone convicted of murder from inheriting from the estate of his victim.

For example, Frank's will contained a provision that Sam, Frank's neighbor, would inherit $20,000 if he would pistol whip Frank's former boss. This is illegal. A will can never be used for this purpose.

Similarly, leaving money in your will to establish a training school for pickpockets, or leaving money to your son on the condition that he never pay income tax, are not legal bequests.

How much to charity?

Most states place restrictions on the amount of money that you can bequeath to charity. If you are survived by a spouse, child or a parent, charitable bequests are often limited to no more than one half of your estate. Charitable bequests made within a certain number of days before death are also limited. Check with your state's laws regarding this issue.

Choosing a probate attorney

You cannot specify in your will which attorney your personal representative may hire to probate your estate. This power to choose a particular attorney is given to the personal representative. However, feel free to let your personal representative know of your strong feelings about the choice of an attorney to probate your will. You should expect your chosen personal representative to cooperate, whenever possible, with your wishes.

Property not included in your will

Property that cannot be included in your will is called *non-probate property*. This refers to the property that is subject to laws or contracts that were made prior to your will and remains under control of those laws or contracts. This property is not considered part of your estate. Six common examples of non-probate property:

1) **Jointly owned property:** Since property is equally owned by the owners, it automatically passes to the other joint owner upon your death. This form of ownership may include your home, bank accounts, stocks and bonds or even your automobile. The owners of this property are often called "joint tenants with the right of survivorship."

2) **Community property:** To understand the theory of asset division in community property states, you must first understand that community property states view marriage as an equal business partnership. The law then divides property into two categories: community property and separate property.

> **Definition:**
> *Tenant* (types of ownership). When referring to renting or leasing, a tenant is that person(s) or company renting the property. When referring to the ownership of property, such as in a will, a tenant is the person or company who owns all or part of a property, as in "joint tenants with right of survivorship."

Community property is anything acquired jointly, or by either spouse, during the marriage. Separate property is from one of two sources:

a) Property that each spouse owned individually before the marriage and retained in his or her name after the marriage.

b) Property that each spouse received as a gift or inheritance either before or during the marriage.

Each spouse's separate property remains separate property and is not subject to division. If you exchange one item of separate property for another, the new property continues as separate property. So too if the proceeds of sale of separate property are used to acquire new property. Caution: If you commingle separate property with joint property, the separate property becomes joint property subject to division. Separate property must always remain separate so it can always be distinguished from joint property.

> *note* There are nine community property states: Arizona, California, Idaho, Louisiana, Nevada, New Mexico, Texas, Washington and Wisconsin.

As with assets, liabilities that either spouse has incurred prior to the marriage remain a separate obligation. While the parties may agree to keep separate debts incurred during the marriage, these provisions do not bind creditors.

How do you best protect your property in a community property state? Start by listing your property when you marry. Clearly stipulate that it is to remain separate property thereafter. Similarly, keep separate any gifts or inheritances you receive during your marriage. These assets will then always remain yours.

3) **Property under contract:** If, for example, you had a contract to sell your home and you died before closing, the buyer could nevertheless enforce the contract. Although the house is not part of the estate, the proceeds of the sale would be.

4) **Life insurance policy:** If the beneficiary of your life insurance policy is a person who is still living, the proceeds from that policy are paid directly to that beneficiary and are not part of your estate. However, if the estate itself is the named beneficiary of your life insurance policy, or if the named beneficiary dies before you do, then the proceeds from the policy will become part of your estate.

5) **Pay-on-death account:** Also known as a Totten Trust, this is a special type of savings account. The depositor is listed as trustee and another person is the beneficiary. The advantage of this type of account is that the depositor may withdraw money from the account at any time during his or her lifetime. When the depositor dies, the money in the account is inherited by the named beneficiary. This money passes directly to the beneficiary and is not part of the depositor's estate.

> **E-Z TIP**
>
> Most often you own your own life insurance policy, which means you must pay the premiums and designate the beneficiary(ies) of your choice. Consider having your spouse, or trusted family member or friend own your policy. You could still pay the premiums and, if they were willing, ask them to choose the beneficiaries you wish. This way, you could avoid paying federal estate taxes upon your death, since you would not actually own the policy.

6) **Property you no longer own:** Such as gifts you made during your lifetime.

7) **Living trust assets:** Most often, property held in a living trust automatically bypasses probate. That is one reason why living trusts are so popular. For information on living trusts and how they can benefit you, check out E-Z Legal's guide, *Living Trusts Made E-Z*.

Definition:

Life estate. A life estate is real estate that is owned for the duration of a person's lifetime.

Life estates, pension plan distributions with beneficiaries who are named, and individual retirement accounts with named beneficiaries are also considered to be non-probate property and should not be included in your estate.

Disinheriting

All states have specific laws (statutes) that deal with disinheritance. When you disinherit someone, you leave him or her nothing in your will.

Disinheriting a spouse

In most states it is, by law, almost impossible to disinherit a spouse completely. Suppose you decided to leave a token gift of one dollar to your spouse. Your spouse would, under most state laws, have the right to reject the dollar inheritance and instead take a state-mandated percentage of the estate. This percentage is called a *forced share* or *elective share*. The court will usually allow the spouse six to nine months to decide whether to take his or her forced share.

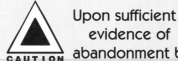

DEFINITION

For example, Tom bequeaths all of his property to his children from a previous marriage. He leaves nothing to his wealthy wife. Under the law, Tom's wife can still receive a fixed percentage (usually about 30 percent) of Tom's estate, and his children share the remainder.

CAUTION Upon sufficient evidence of abandonment by a spouse, some states allow the abandoned spouse to disinherit the departed spouse. A missing spouse, one who has not necessarily abandoned their partner but who has inexplicably disappeared, could not be disinherited and would have to be declared legally dead by a court of law.

Another example, Alice has a joint bank account with her husband. She puts half of her property in this account and states in her will that her brother is to inherit all of her other property when she dies. In fact, when Alice dies her husband receives not only all of the money in the joint account, but also a fixed percentage (about 30 percent) of all the property that Alice willed to her brother. In effect, the state is saying that the law will try to provide for your surviving spouse even if you do not.

In some states a distinction is made between personal property and real estate (or real property). Under certain circumstances, a husband may disinherit his wife from any share in his real property in:

Arizona	Michigan	South Dakota
District of Columbia	North Carolina	Utah
Florida	North Dakota	Wisconsin
Georgia	South Carolina	

A husband, may under certain circumstances, disinherit his wife from any share in his personal property in:

Alaska	Georgia	South Carolina
Arizona	Michigan	South Dakota
Delaware	North Dakota	Utah
Florida	Oregon	Wisconsin
	Rhode Island	

Fewer states grant a wife the right to disinherit a husband. Only North Dakota and South Dakota permit her to disinherit him from a share in her real property. A wife may, however, disinherit a husband from personal property in:

Alaska	New Jersey	South Carolina
Delaware	North Dakota	South Dakota
Georgia	Oregon	Utah
	Rhode Island	

If it is your intention to disinherit your spouse but you are unsure of the laws in your state, you may use this language as an example:

"I leave to my wife, Ellen, absolutely nothing, or, if unlawful to do so, such minimum share of my estate as shall be required by state law."

note In every state but Louisiana, parents may legitimately disinherit their children. And your spouse may be entitled to a certain percentage of your estate, no matter how much (or how little) you left them in your will.

If your spouse signs a valid prenuptial, antenuptial, or pre-marriage agreement waiving any rights to inherit, then you may disinherit that spouse in any state.

Remember, it is often wiser to leave your spouse some bequest so as to avoid a contest over your will.

Disinheriting children

Suppose you want to disinherit children. Should you simply leave them out of your will? It is never advisable to disinherit someone by leaving him or her out of the will. Too often this may appear to be a mistake on your part. It can be argued that you simply forgot to include that person.

CAUTION Any of your beneficiaries or heirs can contest (or challenge the validity of) your will. Be certain you prepare your will correctly and legally, and if you disinherit someone, make certain there are no grounds for declaring the will invalid.

One technique for disinheriting someone is to leave that person a token amount of money or a token gift. By leaving someone one dollar, you are informing the court that you did give some thought to that bequest. If you decide that even one dollar is too much to give that person, you should specifically state in your will that you disinherit that person, name him or her, and if possible explain the reason. Again, this makes it clear to anyone reading the will that you did not leave that person out by mistake. Proper language to disinherit may read:

"Since I have not heard from my son John Smith in over five years, I leave him nothing."

or

"I recognize that my daughter Mary Smith is financially secure, and therefore leave her nothing."

After your will is completed

Chapter 9
After your will is completed

What you'll find in this chapter:

➠ Other forms that go with your will

➠ Storing your will

➠ Attorneys and safe deposit boxes

➠ When there are previous wills

➠ Making copies of your will

Completing additional forms

Besides the Last Will & Testament, you will find additional forms in the back of this guide. These forms contain your suggestions, wishes, and instructions not included in your will. Bear in mind that these documents are not legally binding upon your personal representative, as they are not actually part of your will. Make as many copies of these forms as you need. If you decide to store the forms with your will, give copies to your attorney or personal representative, where they will be kept safe and accessible.

CAUTION Do not make any changes directly on the will after it has been completed, signed and witnessed, because those changes will not be valid. Prepare a codicil (formal addition) to the will, or better yet, make a new will.

Storage and safekeeping

Your will should be stored in a safe but easily accessible place. When it is time for your personal representative to put your estate plan into operation and administer your estate, he or she must have your will in hand. You certainly do not want family members to have to search for your will during a time of grief and anxiety.

EZ TIP: Be careful about putting your will in a safety deposit box. Some states seal safety deposit boxes immediately upon death, making it impossible to locate the will and increasing the time and money involved to probate your estate. It also may be difficult for a spouse or family member to obtain access to your box without cooperation from the bank.

There are four recommended locations to store your original will. Whichever you choose, it's a good idea to store a copy of your will in at least one of the other places mentioned below:

1) **Probate court or registry of wills.** Find out if your state permits a testator to register a will with the probate court or registry of wills. If so, deposit your original will there so that it will always be on file. The only drawback to doing this is that you have to return to the court every time you want to update your will.

2) **Your attorney.** You may deposit your original will with an attorney. Attorneys often agree to store your will for free, as this increases the likelihood that you will use their services in the future.

3) **Safe deposit box.** You may store your will in a safe deposit box. Even if the box is sealed upon the death of the testator, as a matter of law or general practice, the bank may allow a personal representative or member of the immediate family to gain access to the safe deposit box in order to

retrieve the will. Since the will must be probated anyway, and there should be at least one copy elsewhere, a sealed safe deposit box should not present an insurmountable problem.

Perhaps a more common-sense approach is to place your will in a safe deposit box rented in your spouse's name, and keep your spouse's will in a safe deposit box rented in your name. In this way, each will is immediately available to the other spouse, even if the box of the deceased spouse has been sealed.

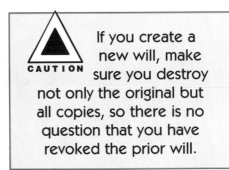

If you create a new will, make sure you destroy not only the original but all copies, so there is no question that you have revoked the prior will.

4) **Friend, relative, or personal representative.** You may leave your will with a trusted friend, relative or the personal representative of your estate.

Do not store your will on a computer disk as it must be printed, signed and witnessed to be valid.

Sometimes, after a person's death, more than one will is found, and often these wills contradict each other. Because you can only have one valid will, the court uses the date of the will as the determining factor. The last dated will is presumed to be the valid will that will govern your estate. Always destroy old wills to avoid any confusion.

Wherever you choose to deposit your original will, make sure that copies are accessible. Keep accurate records of where your will and copies are located, and give this information to your personal representative.

The eternal will

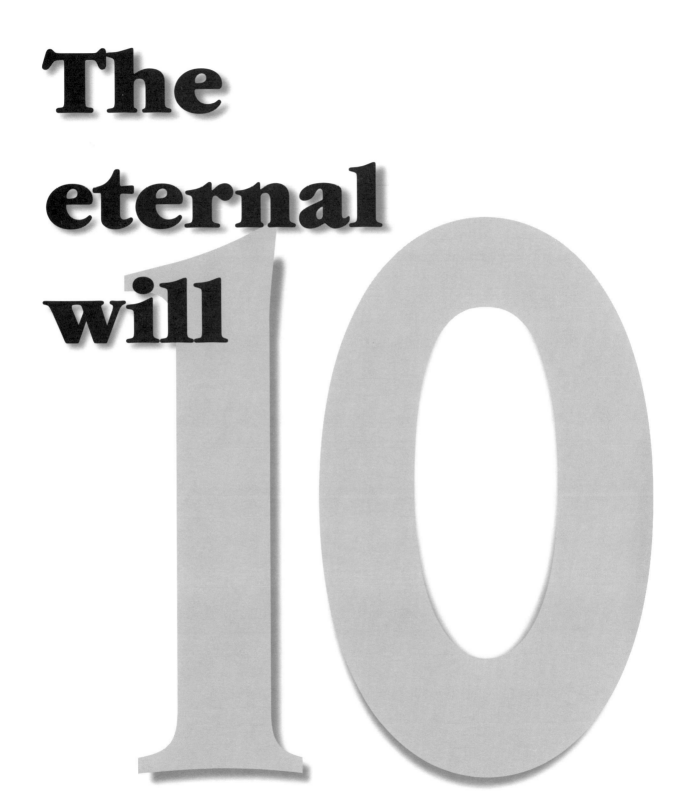

Chapter 10

The eternal will

After preparing your will, you may wonder how long it will remain valid or how soon you must prepare a new one. There are three occasions when the law automatically revokes your will:

1) **You intentionally destroy your will.** Destroying a will includes intentionally burning, tearing, canceling or obliterating it. Accidental destruction of a will does not cancel it. If your will is destroyed by an accidental fire in your home, a copy of the signed original may be offered to the court as evidence of your intention. It is presumed that if you had wanted to destroy your will, you would have also destroyed the copies.

2) **You change your will without following legal procedure.** Never simply make changes or alter the terms of your will. If you want to make changes, there are two legally accepted ways:

a. *Prepare a codicil.* A codicil is a legal supplement and can be used to add or remove anything from your will. But don't be fooled by this simple statement. A codicil must meet the same requirements as a will, and must also have the same number of witnesses. Therefore, it is often less complicated to simply prepare a new will, rather than to add a codicil.

> *note* J. Paul Getty, one of the world's richest men drafted no less than 21 separate codicils between 1960 and 1976 with each codicil canceling its predecessor. Could there be a 22nd?

b. *Prepare a new will.* This gives you the opportunity to reconsider all of the provisions in your will and to make all of the changes at one time. Be sure to state in your will that it revokes or cancels all prior wills and codicils that you have made. Otherwise, the court may treat it as an amendment and not as a replacement.

3) **An operation of law, such as marriage or divorce, cancels your will.**

a. *Marriage.* Unless your will specifically states that you were planning on marriage when you made your will, it will be revoked upon your marriage in these nine states:

Connecticut	Kentucky
Georgia	Massachusetts
New Hampshire	Oregon
Rhode Island	West Virginia
Wisconsin	

For example, Bob bequeathed all of his property to his brother. Although Bob subsequently married Susan, a wealthy debutante, Bob never changed his will because he still wanted his brother to inherit his money. But Bob's marriage to Susan automatically revoked his will, and technically, he died without a will. Susan inherited his entire estate and Bob's brother received nothing.

In California, Nevada and Washington, your will is not revoked upon your marriage, but bequests made to your former spouse are canceled.

In Delaware, Kansas, Louisiana, Maryland, Oklahoma and Tennessee your entire will is revoked if and when a child is born of a new marriage.

Marriage has no effect upon a will in the following states:

Alabama	Alaska	Arizona
Arkansas	Colorado	Florida
Hawaii	Idaho	Illinois
Indiana	Iowa	Louisiana
Maine	Michigan	Minnesota
Mississippi	Missouri	Montana
Nebraska	New Jersey	New Mexico
New York	North Carolina	North Dakota
Ohio	Pennsylvania	South Carolina
Texas	Utah	Vermont
Virginia	Wyoming	

As of this printing, the preceding and the following information about specific states is true. You should check your individual state's laws for updated information.

b. *Divorce.* If you become divorced in Connecticut, Georgia or West Virginia, your will is revoked. A divorce does not revoke your will in the following states, but it does revoke bequests made to a former spouse:

Alabama	Alaska	Arizona
Arkansas	California	Colorado
Delaware	Florida	Hawaii
Idaho	Illinois	Indiana
Kansas	Kentucky	Maine
Maryland	Massachusetts	Michigan
Minnesota	Missouri	Montana
Nebraska	Nevada	New Jersey
New Mexico	New York	North Carolina
North Dakota	Ohio	Oklahoma
Oregon	Pennsylvania	Rhode Island
South Carolina	South Dakota	Tennessee
Texas	Utah	Virginia
Washington	Wisconsin	Wyoming

A divorce has no effect on a will in these states:

Iowa	Louisiana	Mississippi
New Hampshire		Vermont

Again, you should check your state's statutes for updated laws.

Other times to change a will

Intentional destruction of your will, changing your will, a new marriage or a divorce are clear signals that you must prepare a new will. Keep in mind that it may also be a wise decision to prepare a new will if:

- There is a significant change in your financial condition or if your will contains bequests of items that you no longer own.

- A minor child reaches adulthood, is emancipated, or is married, and is able to take responsibility for him or herself without a legal guardian.

> **Definition:**
> *Annulment.* With an annulment, the court declares that your marriage had never occurred in the first place. It is not a divorce, so there is no reason to make a new will after an annulled marriage. By law, no marriage ever took place to revoke the original will.

- There are family additions, such as the birth or adoption of a child. Here you may decide to appoint a guardian and include the child in your will.

- There are changes in the federal or state tax laws. Changes in your tax bracket, deductions or exemptions can have a dramatic impact upon your estate. It is a sound idea to review your will every year at tax time.

- Your personal relationships change. As old friendships fade away and you make new ones, or as loved ones' needs change, you may want to change your beneficiaries.

- A beneficiary and/or the alternate beneficiary dies before you do.

- You move to another state. A change in your permanent residence affects how your will may be administered.

A new will, written in the state where you currently live, is easier to administer. Your will also helps to establish your legal residence.

Unless any of the foregoing circumstances occur, your will continues to be valid for an unlimited time.

> **note**
>
> Like a will, a prenuptial, ante-nuptial, or premarriage agreement not only addresses the division of property, but also things such as insurance, pension plans, and children. A prenuptial agreement could help in determining ownership should one party die without a valid will. You can also create a postnuptial agreement after marriage, which would accomplish the same thing.

Wills, past and present

Since the first formal, legal will was created, the language and the legalese may have evolved, but the last will and testament has changed surprisingly little in form and format. People hundreds of years ago were bequeathing their property to family members and friends as carefully and specifically as we do today—proof that no matter what property you own, how wealthy you may be, and how many beneficiaries you choose, a will is still a will, and everyone needs one.

To give you an example, here's a will nearly 400 years old:

The Will of Martin Christian, 1615

In the name of God, Amen. I Martin Christen of Pevemsey in the County of Sussex, being sicke and weake in body and in good remembraunce thanks bee to God, doe ordayne this my last will and Testament in manner and forme followinge.

That is to say ffirst I committ my Soule into the Hands of Almighty God my maker and Redeemer and my body to te earth in Christian buryalls. And concerninge my land, goods and chattels I will and give unto my sonne John and heyres for ever my Crofte of Land in Pevemsey called Gregs Crofte, which I lately purchased of ffrauncis Normun and Zabulon Newington, uppon condition that hee the sayd John shall paye unto my sonne Abraham his youngest brother fyfteene pounds when the said Abraham shall attayne the Age of One and Twenty years.

Item: I give unto my sonne Stephen and his heyres for ever my dwelling howse barne and crofte of lande thereto belonging with the appurtenaunts uppon condition that he shall paye to my sayd sonne Abraham six pounds when he shall accomplish the age of Three and Twenty years. Provided that if my sonne Stephen shall dye before hee shall attayne to the sayd age of One and Twenty years, my will is that Abraham shall have the sayd howse barn and crofte.

Item: My will is that I enioyne the sayd Stephen if he live, or the sayd Abraham if Stephen dye before the sayd age, to paye my twoe daughters Sara and Mary Ten pounds a peece at their severall ages of One and Twenty years and the one to be the others heyres if eyther of them dye before. Item: My mynde and will is that if I dye of this sicknes my wife shall have the crofte given to John whole rent free for one yeare after my decease and her dwelling in the house and use and proffitt of the same and barne and crofte untill Stephen attayne to the age of Three and Twenty years. Item: I give unto my sonne John one cupbord and one ioyned chest. Also I give to eache of my three sonnes A pewter platter.

All the rest of my goods and chattles unbequeathed, my debts payd and funerall expenses dischardged, I bequeath to Dorathye my wife whom I make sole Executrix of this my Last Will and Testament and ordayne Richard Cockshott and John Walcock my Overseers. Also, my will is that, whereas above sayd I have appoynted my sonne John to pay to my sonne Abraham fyfteene pounds if Stephen shall dye before he come to this age aforesayd that Abraham enioye the lande, then Tenn pounds of the fifteene shalbee ugually devided between my twoe daughters and the five pounds to remayne with John. Also, I give to my Overseers in token of love three shillings four pence a peece.

Dated this thirde day of August One Thousand six hundred and fyf-teene. The marke of Martin Christen Witnesses hereof Richard Cockshott his mark John Walcock his marke George Wilborke.

Proved 29th August 1615. Archdeaconry of Lewes

Probate to Dorathy Christian, Relict

Suppose I change my mind?

 Your will is a legal document that can be changed. Any property that you bequeath is property that you still own up to the time of your death. As such, you have the right to sell, destroy, abandon, make a gift of or distribute it in any manner that you see fit. Remember, a will only becomes effective upon your death.

For example, the bequest that "I leave to my brother Jack my 1992 Cadillac sedan" means that your brother Jack inherits your 1992 Cadillac sedan only if you own it at the time of your death. If you traded your Cadillac for a 1997 Mercedes, your brother would not receive the

> *note* If your previously canceled will is replaced by an invalid one, the canceled will is held to be the valid one. This prevents the person from dying intestate.

Mercedes in its place. If you decide to give Jack your Cadillac while you are still living, your gift cancels the Cadillac left to him in your will.

Of course, an up-to-date will reflects your latest wishes more clearly and is easier to administer. If your will contains several bequests that are no longer possible, it is time to add a codicil or write a new will. You should review your will on a regular basis. Mark the time for reviewing your will on your calendar, or do it every October—National Will Month.

Probate

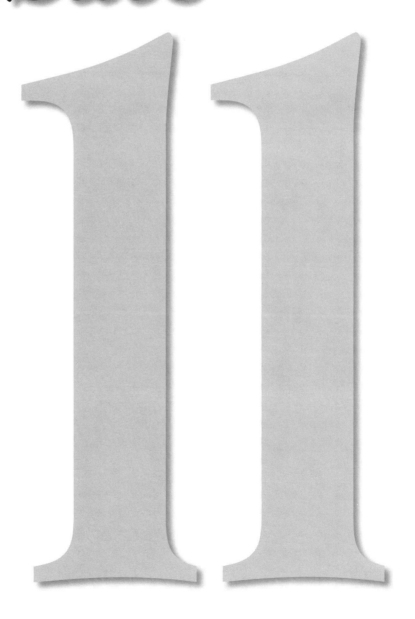

Chapter 11

Probate

What you'll find in this chapter:

➡ The mystery of probate

➡ The different types of probate

➡ Contesting a will

➡ Problems you may have with probate

➡ Once your will is accepted

What is probate?

Probate is the process by which the court gives its official approval to your will and your personal representative is appointed. Upon your death, your will is submitted to the court by your personal representative. The court determines that signatures are genuine, that you were free from delusions when you made the will, and that you were not pressured, threatened or tricked into making it or forced to alter any of the terms of the will. The court also examines your choice of personal representative as to

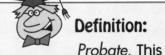

Definition:

Probate. This literally means "proof of a will;" probate court is the entity that processes the estate of a deceased person; probate estate is all of a person's assets that go through probate.

---

his or her character and past. If your will meets the requirements of the court, it is admitted. The court officially appoints the personal representative that you have chosen, and instructs him or her to carry out the terms of your will. This allows your personal representative to distribute and liquidate your property and to take any necessary legal actions on your behalf.

Types of probate

There are two types of probate process: formal and informal.

Formal probate requires that anyone who may have an interest in the will, including creditors of the estate, be notified in advance, usually within thirty days of the reading of the will, so they may challenge the validity of the will and/or the appointment of the personal representative.

Formal proceedings generally involve ten steps:

1) A formal petition to admit the will to probate is filed with the court.

2) All interested parties are given notice.

3) If there is a will, the will is recognized by the court as genuine.

4) Unless waived, the personal representative posts bond.

5) The court issues letters of administration.

6) The personal representative files an inventory with the court.

7) The creditors are given notice of time allotted to present claims against the estate.

8) All taxes, debts, and expenses of the estate are paid.

9) Beneficiaries receive their distributions.

10)   The personal representative files a final account with the court.

Informal probate may be conducted when the assets of the deceased's estate are below a certain value determined by state statute or when there is no reason for the court to supervise the entire process of settling the estate. Persons with an interest in the will are not notified and the clerk of the court acts as the registrar, voluntary executor, or voluntary administrator. Thus, it is a relatively simple process with a minimum of paperwork. In some states, informal probate is known as independent probate or probate in common form.

Probate is protection

The process of probate is necessary to protect both your wishes and your beneficiaries. One of the most important functions of probate is to make sure that the document you are submitting as your Last Will & Testament is really your last one. The court has to be sure that there is no other will that you wrote to replace the one submitted to the court.

Remember, a will can be changed at any time up to your death. We have all read about famous probate cases in which large estates could never be distributed to the beneficiaries because there was no reliable way to determine which document was the last will.

Contesting a will

Under certain circumstances, a will may be contested by any beneficiary or heir. To contest a will, the person must prove that he or she would lose a benefit if the will was allowed. Grounds for contesting a will include proving:

• that the will was not properly filled out

• that the testator was of unsound mind

- that there was fraud involved

- that the testator did something contrary to his or her real wishes and desires.

The burden of proof is always upon the person contesting the will.

Undue influence

To contest a will on the grounds of undue influence, one must prove

- undue influence was exerted on the testator

- the intention of the undue influence was to overpower the testator's mind and will

- the result of the undue influence was the creation of a will, codicil or provision to a will that is clearly not the intention of the testator but of the influencing party(ies) using the following evidence:

note Just in case you were considering it, you cannot inherit from your parents if you are found guilty of their murder. Spouses who are found guilty of their mate's murder receive only their share of jointly owned property, and have no rights to anything owned solely by the deceased spouse.

- ◆ the testator was physically or mentally weak

- ◆ opportunity of the influencing party(ies)

- ◆ the outcome of the will greatly favors the influencing party(ies).

Special problems in probate

There are certain situations that cause special problems when an estate is probated. Should you find yourself with one of these problems, seek the advice of an attorney. These situations include, but are not limited to, the following:

- illegal acts, including committing murder to benefit from the deceased's will

- abandonment by a spouse

- missing spouse

- artificial insemination issues

Finally . . .

Once your Last Will & Testament has been accepted by the court, the probate process ensures that your beneficiaries receive their inheritances exactly as you instructed. Most states provide a family allowance to take care of the surviving spouse and minor children until probate is completed. This amounts to an advance against what the family will inherit under the will.

The forms in this guide

About These E-Z Legal Forms:
While the legal forms and documents in this product generally conform to the requirements of courts nationwide, certain courts may have additional requirements. Before completing and filing the forms in this product, check with the clerk of the court concerning these requirements.

LAST WILL AND TESTAMENT
OF

JOHN DOE

BE IT KNOWN that I, John Doe , a resident of Anytown , County of Douglas , in the State of California , being of sound mind, do make and declare this to be my Last Will and Testament expressly revoking all my prior Wills and Codicils at any time made.

I.   PERSONAL REPRESENTATIVE:

I appoint Mary Doe of Anytown, California , as Personal Representative of this my Last Will and Testament and provide if this Personal Representative is unable or unwilling to serve then I appoint William Smith of Anytown, California , as alternate Personal Representative. My Personal Representative shall be authorized to carry out all provisions of this Will and pay my just debts, obligations and funeral expenses. I further provide my Personal Representative shall not be required to post surety bond in this or any other jurisdiction, and direct that no expert appraisal be made of my estate unless required by law.

II.   GUARDIAN:

In the event I shall die as the sole parent of minor children, then I appoint Elizabeth Morris as Guardian of said minor children. If this named Guardian is unable or unwilling to serve, then I appoint Martha Smith as alternate Guardian.

III.   BEQUESTS:

I direct that after payment of all my just debts, my property be bequeathed in the manner following:

1. I bequeath my gun collection to my brother, Henry Doe.

2. I bequeath the sum of $20,000 to Anytown College, to use in such manner as it deems proper.

3. All the rest and residue of my property, of every nature and description, I leave said property to my wife, Mary Doe. If she should predecease me, I leave said property to my son Charles, and if shall also pre- decease me, then to his surviving children equally.

John Doe
Testator Signature

Page 1 of 2 .

Execute and attest before a notary.
Caution: Louisiana residents should consult an attorney before preparing a will.

IN WITNESS WHEREOF, I have hereunto set my hand this   2nd   day of
January   , 1992 (year), to this my Last Will and Testament.

_____*John Doe*_____
Testator Signature

IV.   WITNESSED:

The testator has signed this will at the end and on each other separate page, and has declared or signified in our presence that it is his/her last will and testament, and in the presence of the testator and each other we have hereunto subscribed our names this 2nd day of   January   , 1992   (year).

_____*Anne Blake*_____   5 Clark Street, Anytown, CA
Witness Signature   Address

_____*William Compton*_____   300 Main Street, Anytown, CA
Witness Signature   Address

_____*Harry Jones*_____   11 Smith Avenue, Anytown, CA
Witness Signature   Address

ACKNOWLEDGMENT

State of   California   }
County of   Douglas
We, _____John Doe_____, _____Anne Blake_____,
_____William Compton_____, and _____Harry Jones_____,
the testator and the witnesses, respectively, whose names are signed to the attached and foregoing instrument, were sworn and declared to the undersigned that the testator signed the instrument as his/her Last Will and Testament and that each of the witnesses, in the presence of the testator and each other, signed the will as witnesses.

Testator: *John Doe*   Witness: *Anne Blake*
                                        Witness: *William Compton*
                                        Witness: *Harry Jones*

On January 2, 1992 before me,   Nick Notary   ,
appeared   John Doe, Anne Blake, William Compton, and Harry Jones
personally known to me (or proved to me on the basis of satisfactory evidence) to be the person(s) whose name(s) is/are subscribed to the within instrument and acknowledged to me that he/she/they executed the same in his/her/their authorized capacity(ies), and that by his/her/their signature(s) on the instrument the person(s), or the entity upon behalf of which the person(s) acted, executed the instrument.
WITNESS my hand and official seal.

Signature_____*Nick Notary*_____

Affiant   ✔ Known_____Produced ID
Type of ID Driver's License

(Seal)

LAST WILL AND TESTAMENT
OF

       BE IT KNOWN that I,   , a resident of   , County of   , in the State of   , being of sound mind, do make and declare this to be my Last Will and Testament expressly revoking all my prior Wills and Codicils at any time made.

I.   PERSONAL REPRESENTATIVE:

       I appoint   of   , as Personal Representative of this my Last Will and Testament and provide if this Personal Representative is unable or unwilling to serve then I appoint   of   , as alternate Personal Representative. My Personal Representative shall be authorized to carry out all provisions of this Will and pay my just debts, obligations and funeral expenses. I further provide my Personal Representative shall not be required to post surety bond in this or any other jurisdiction, and direct that no expert appraisal be made of my estate unless required by law.

II.   GUARDIAN:

       In the event I shall die as the sole parent of minor children, then I appoint   as Guardian of said minor children. If this named Guardian is unable or unwilling to serve, then I appoint   as alternate Guardian.

III.   BEQUESTS:

       I direct that after payment of all my just debts, my property be bequeathed in the manner following:

_____

Testator's Initials

Page ____ of ____.

Execute and attest before a notary.
Caution: Louisiana residents should consult an attorney before preparing a will.

Page _____ of _____.

_____

Testator's Initials

Page _____ of _____.

IN WITNESS WHEREOF, I have hereunto set my hand this _____ day of _____ , _____ (year), to this my Last Will and Testament.

_____
Testator Signature

IV.   **WITNESSED:**

       The testator has signed this will at the end and on each other separate page, and has declared or signified in our presence that it is his/her last will and testament, and in the presence of the testator and each other we have hereunto subscribed our names this _____ day of _____ , _____ (year).

_____   _____
Witness Signature   Address

_____   _____
Witness Signature   Address

_____   _____
Witness Signature   Address

ACKNOWLEDGMENT

State of _____
County of _____   }

We, _____ , _____ ,

_____ , and _____ ,

the testator and the witnesses, respectively, whose names are signed to the attached and foregoing instrument, were sworn and declared to the undersigned that the testator signed the instrument as his/her Last Will and Testament and that each of the witnesses, in the presence of the testator and each other, signed the will as witnesses.

Testator: _____   Witness: _____

                                                  Witness: _____

                                                  Witness: _____

On _____ before me, _____ ,
appeared _____
personally known to me (or proved to me on the basis of satisfactory evidence) to be the person(s) whose name(s) is/are subscribed to the within instrument and acknowledged to me that he/she/they executed the same in his/her/their authorized capacity(ies), and that by his/her/their signature(s) on the instrument the person(s), or the entity upon behalf of which the person(s) acted, executed the instrument.
WITNESS my hand and official seal.

Signature_____

                                         Affiant   _____Known_____Produced ID
                                         Type of ID_____
                                                      (Seal)

Page _____ of _____.

SCHEDULE OF ASSETS

Name of Testator:_____ Date of Will:_____

No.	Description of item	Form of ownership	Replacement cost
_____	_____	_____	_____
_____	_____	_____	_____
_____	_____	_____	_____
_____	_____	_____	_____
_____	_____	_____	_____
_____	_____	_____	_____
_____	_____	_____	_____
_____	_____	_____	_____
_____	_____	_____	_____
_____	_____	_____	_____
_____	_____	_____	_____
_____	_____	_____	_____
_____	_____	_____	_____
_____	_____	_____	_____
_____	_____	_____	_____
_____	_____	_____	_____
_____	_____	_____	_____
_____	_____	_____	_____
_____	_____	_____	_____
_____	_____	_____	_____
_____	_____	_____	_____
_____	_____	_____	_____
_____	_____	_____	_____
_____	_____	_____	_____

INSURANCE/PENSION DATA

LIFE INSURANCE POLICIES

Company :_____

Agent:_____ Telephone: _____

Policy Number:_____ Date:_____

Amount:_____ Owner:_____

Location of Policy:_____

Beneficiary:_____

Company :_____

Agent:_____ Telephone: _____

Policy Number:_____ Date:_____

Amount:_____ Owner:_____

Location of Policy:_____

Beneficiary:_____

Company :_____

Agent:_____ Telephone: _____

Policy Number:_____ Date:_____

Amount:_____ Owner:_____

Location of Policy:_____

Beneficiary:_____

PENSIONS/ANNUITIES

Company:_____

Contract:_____ Telephone:_____

Company:_____

Contract:_____ Telephone:_____

DOCUMENT LOCATOR

OF

_____

Insurance Documents: _____

Birth Certificate: _____

Statement of Wishes: _____

Marriage License or Certificate: _____

Social Security Cards: _____

Military Records: _____

Divorce Decree: _____

Mortgage Documents: _____

Bank Passbooks: _____

Passport(s): _____

Tax Returns: _____

Will(s) and Trust(s): _____

Pre-Nuptial Agreement: _____

Business Papers: _____

Death Certificates: _____

Warranties: _____

Stock Certificates: _____

Other Investment Certificates: _____

Letters of Final Request: _____

Anatomical Gift Authorization: _____

Citizenship Papers: _____

Safe Deposit Keys: _____

Financial Records: _____

Other:

_____ : _____

_____ : _____

_____ : _____

_____ : _____

_____ : _____

_____ : _____

NOTIFICATION LIST

Accountant: _____

_____

Attorney: _____

_____

Banker: _____

_____

Clergyman: _____

_____

Executor:

_____

_____

Contingent Executor: _____

_____

Funeral Director: _____

_____

Guardian: _____

_____

Contingent Guardian: _____

_____

Insurance Agent: _____

_____

Insurance Underwriter: _____

_____

FUNERAL REQUESTS

OF

_____

Funeral Home: _____

Director: _____Telephone: _____

Address: _____

Service Type: Religious: _____Military: _____Fraternal: _____

Person Officiating: _____Telephone: _____

Music Selections: _____

Reading Selections: _____

Flowers: _____

Memorials: _____

Pallbearers: _____

Disposition: Burial: _____ Cremation: _____

Other Instructions: _____

_____

BURIAL

Cemetery: _____

Location: _____

Section: _____Plot No.: _____Block: _____

Location of Deed: _____

Special Instructions: _____

FUNERAL EXPENSES COVERAGE

Life Insurance: _____

Social Security: _____Veteran's Administration: _____

Union Benefit: _____Fraternal Organization(s): _____

Pension Benefit: _____

Burial Insurance: _____

PERSONAL INFORMATION

Full Legal Name:_____

Address: _____

Social Security No.: _____Spouse:_____

Medicare No.: _____Spouse:_____

Armed Forces Service No.: _____

Date and Location of Discharge: _____

Birth Date: _____Marriage Date: _____

Father's Full Name: _____

Mother's Full Maiden Name: _____

Widowed:_____Separated: _____Divorced:_____Date:_____

Location of Separation Agreement/Divorce Decree: _____

_____

Remarried? Yes _____No _____   Date:_____

Children:

Name	Address	Birth Date
_____	_____	_____
_____	_____	_____
_____	_____	_____
_____	_____	_____

WILL

Location of Original Last Will:_____

_____Date: _____

Codicil Completed? Yes _____No _____If Yes, Location:_____

_____Date: _____

Location of Any Documents Mentioned in Will: _____

_____Date: _____

STATEMENT OF WISHES
OF

_____

     I,   , do hereby set forth certain wishes and requests to my personal representatives, heirs, family, friends and others who may carry out these wishes. I understand that these wishes are advisory only and not mandatory.

     My wishes are:

Dated:

_____

Signature

Glossary of useful terms

A-B

Administer

To manage your estate until all of the terms of the will are carried out.

Affidavit

A sworn statement under oath.

Alternate

A contingent beneficiary or substitute representative, named to serve in case the original cannot.

Assets

Anything you own that has value.

Beneficiary

A person who inherits from you through your will. A beneficiary may also be a charity or an institution.

Bequest

A gift of property that you make in your will.

Bond

Money paid to the court by the personal representative to ensure that he or she will administer the estate in good faith.

C-E

Codicil

An amendment to the will that changes the will in some way.

Contingent beneficiary

An alternate beneficiary.

Defame

To cause someone embarrassment or humiliation which results in a damaged reputation.

Devise

A gift of real estate, also called a bequest.

Disinherit

To deprive someone of the right to inherit in your will.

Elective share

Also called the forced share, it is the percentage of the estate that the spouse may choose instead of inheriting under the will.

Encumbrance

A legal claim, such as a mortgage, that might block the transfer of property.

Estate

All of the personal and real property that you own at death.

Executor/Executrix

Male and female terms for the person who executes one's will.

G-N

Guardian

The person you name to legally care for your minor children.

Gift

Any bequest that you make in your will.

Inheritance

The gift you receive from a will.

Intestacy

Dying without a valid will.

Legal age

The age at which a minor becomes an adult. This age varies according to state law.

Libel

False written statements about another person.

Living will

A document in which you indicate at what point you no longer want medical science to prolong your life.

Nonmarital child

A child born out of wedlock.

Non-probate property

Property that is not considered to be part of your estate.

Notary

A person authorized by the state to witness and guarantee a signature.

O-T

Operation of law

The rights and obligations that are set forth in the law; marriage and divorce, for example. These rights and obligations do not depend upon private agreements.

Personal representative

The person named in your will to administer your estate.

Probate

The process of proving in court that a will is valid and legal.

Personal property

All of the property you own, excluding real estate; also called personalty.

Real property

All the real estate you own; also called realty. Real property does not include any personal property.

Residuary bequests

The remaining property that has not been distributed elsewhere in the will.

Revoke

To cancel.

Spouse

One's husband or wife; any married person.

Testator

The person making the will if a male.

T-W

Testatrix

The person making the will if a female.

Trust

An agreement whereby one person (grantor) transfers property to a second person (trustee) to be held for the benefit of a third person (beneficiary).

Valid

Legally sound, authentic.

Viatical

A financial service for the terminally ill which enables qualified individuals to obtain immediate cash from all or part of their life insurance policies.

Witness

One who signs his or her name to a will in order to authenticate it.

Resources

••• Wills •••

◆ **ABA Law Practice Management Section—Estate Planning and Probate Interest Group**

URL: http://www.abanet.org/lpm/lpdiv/estate.html

◆ **An Adoptive Child's Right to Inherit**

URL: http://www.scottsdalelaw.com/adoptive.html

◆ **California Estate Planning, Probate & Trust Law**

URL: http://www.ca-probate.com

◆ **Choice in Dying**

    URL: http://www.choices.org

◆ **CPA Journal on Line: Avoiding probate**

    URL: http://www.luca.com/cpajournal/old/16531680.htm

◆ **Crash Course in Wills and Trusts**

    URL: http://www.mtpalermo.com

◆ **Discovering and Obtaining Death Benefits**

    URL: http://www.bluefin.net/~jtcmac

◆ **Estate Planning for Unmarried Couples**

    URL: http://www.trustwizard.com/unmar.htm

◆ **Estate Planning Links Web Site, The**

    URL: http://hometown.aol.com/dmk58/eplinks.html

◆ **Estate Project For Artists With AIDS/HIV**

    URL: http://www.artistswithaids.org

◆ **FAQ on Wills From Teahan & Constantino**

URL: *http://www1.mhv.net/~teahan/willfaq.htm*

◆ **FindLaw**

URL: *http://www.findlaw.com/01topics/31probate*

◆ **Growth House, Inc.**

URL: *http://www.growthhouse.org*

◆ **Law & Estate Planning Sites on the Internet**

URL: *http://www.ca-probate.com/links.htm*

◆ **Law Journal Extra!**

URL: *http://www.ljx.com/practice/trusts/index.html*

◆ **Law Offices of Alvin E. Prather**

URL: *http://www.pratherlaw.com/legalese.html*

◆ **Legal Information Institute**

URL: *http://www.law.cornell.edu/topics/*

state_statutes .html#probate

◆ **'Lectric Law Library™**

URL: *http://www.lectlaw.com*

◆ **National Association of Financial and Estate Planning**

URL: *http://www.nafep.com*

◆ **Robert Clofine's Estate Planning Page**

URL: *http://www.estateattorney.com*

◆ **Ralf's 'Lectric Law Library™ Tour**

URL: *http://www.lectlaw.com/formb.htm*

◆ **Wills on the Web**

URL: *http://www.ca-probate.com/wills.htm*

◆ **World Wide Web Virtual Library: Law: Property Law**

URL: *http://www.law.indiana.edu/law/v-lib/property.html*

••• Viatical Settlements •••

A viatical settlement is a financial service for the terminally ill which enables qualified individuals to obtain immediate cash from all or part of their life insurance policies.

◆ **Better Business Bureau: Tips for Consumers: Viatical Settlements**

URL: http://www.bbb.org/library/viatical.html

◆ **National Viatical Association**

http://www.nationalviatical.org

◆ **Viatical Association Of America, The**

URL: http://www.cais.net/viatical

◆ **Viatical Settlements: A Guide for People with Terminal Illnesses**

URL: http://www.ftc.gov/bcp/conline/pubs/services/viatical.htm

···Related Sites···

◆ **Institute of Certified Financial Planners**

URL: http://www.icfp.org

◆ **International Association for Financial Planning**

URL: http://www.iafp.org

◆ **MSN MoneyCentral**

URL: http://www.moneycentral.com/retire/home.asp

◆ **National Association of Personal Financial Advisors**

URL: http://www.napfa.org

◆ **Pension and Welfare Benefits Administration**

URL: http://www.dol.gov/dol/pwba

••• Legal Search Engines •••

◆ **All Law**

http://www.alllaw.com

◆ **American Law Sources On Line**

http://www.lawsource.com/also/searchfm.htm

◆ **Catalaw**

http://www.catalaw.com

◆ **FindLaw**

URL: http://www.findlaw.com

◆ **Hieros Gamos**

http://www.hg.org/hg.html

◆ **InternetOracle**

http://www.internetoracle.com/legal.htm

◆ **LawAid**

http://www.lawaid.com/search.html

◆ **LawCrawler**

http://www.lawcrawler.com

◆ **LawEngine, The**

http://www.fastsearch.com/law

◆ **LawRunner**

http://www.lawrunner.com

◆ **'Lectric Law Library™**

URL: http://www.lectlaw.com

◆ **Legal Search Engines**

http://www.dreamscape.com/frankvad/search.legal.html

◆ **LEXIS/NEXIS Communications Center**

http://www.lexis-nexis.com/lncc/general/search.html

◆ **Meta-Index for U.S. Legal Research**

http://gsulaw.gsu.edu/metaindex

◆ **Seamless Website, The**

http://seamless.com

◆ **USALaw**

http://www.usalaw.com/linksrch.cfm

◆ **WestLaw**

http://westdoc.com

(Registered users only. Fee paid service.)

••• State Bar Associations •••

ALABAMA

Alabama State Bar
415 Dexter Avenue
Montgomery, AL 36104

mailing address:
PO Box 671
Montgomery, AL 36101
(205) 269-1515

http://www.alabar.org

ALASKA

Alaska Bar Association
510 L Street No. 602
Anchorage, AK 99501

mailing address
PO Box 100279
Anchorage, AK 99510

ARIZONA

State Bar of Arizona
111 West Monroe
Phoenix, AZ 85003-1742
(602) 252-4804

ARKANSAS

Arkansas Bar Association
400 West Markham
Little Rock, AR 72201
(501) 375-4605

CALIFORNIA

State Bar of California
555 Franklin Street
San Francisco, CA 94102
(415) 561-8200

http://www.calbar.org
Alameda County Bar
Association

http://www.acbanet.org

COLORADO

Colorado Bar Association
No. 950, 1900 Grant Street
Denver, CO 80203
(303) 860-1115

http://www.cobar.org

CONNECTICUT

Connecticut Bar Association
101 Corporate Place
Rocky Hill, CT 06067-1894
(203) 721-0025

DELAWARE

Delaware State Bar Association
1225 King Street, 10th floor
Wilmington, DE 19801
(302) 658-5279
(302) 658-5278 (lawyer referral service)

DISTRICT OF COLUMBIA

District of Columbia Bar
1250 H Street, NW, 6th Floor
Washington, DC 20005
(202) 737-4700

Bar Association of the District of
Columbia
1819 H Street, NW, 12th floor
Washington, DC 20006-3690
(202) 223-6600

FLORIDA

The Florida Bar
The Florida Bar Center
650 Apalachee Parkway
Tallahassee, FL 32399-2300
(904) 561-5600

GEORGIA

State Bar of Georgia
800 The Hurt Building
50 Hurt Plaza
Atlanta, GA 30303
(404) 527-8700

http://www.gabar.org

HAWAII

Hawaii State Bar Association
1136 Union Mall
Penthouse 1
Honolulu, HI 96813
(808) 537-1868

http://www.hsba.org

IDAHO

Idaho State Bar
PO Box 895
Boise, ID 83701
(208) 334-4500

ILLINOIS

Illinois State Bar Association
424 South Second Street
Springfield, IL 62701
(217) 525-1760

INDIANA

Indiana State Bar Association
230 East Ohio Street
Indianapolis, IN 46204
(317) 639-5465

http://www.iquest.net/isba

IOWA

Iowa State Bar Association
521 East Locust
Des Moines, IA 50309
(515) 243-3179

http://www.iowabar.org

KANSAS

Kansas Bar Association
1200 Harrison Street
Topeka, KS 66601
(913) 234-5696

http://www.ink.org/public/
cybar

KENTUCKY

Kentucky Bar Association
514 West Main Street
Frankfort, KY 40601-1883
(502) 564-3795

http://www.kybar.org

LOUISIANA

Louisiana State Bar Association
601 St. Charles Avenue
New Orleans, LA 70130
(504) 566-1600

MAINE

Maine State Bar Association
124 State Street
PO Box 788
Augusta, ME 04330
(207) 622-7523

http://www.mainebar.org

MARYLAND

Maryland State Bar Association
520 West Fayette Street
Baltimore, MD 21201
(410) 685-7878

http://www.msba.org/msba

MASSACHUSETTS

Massachusetts Bar Association
20 West Street
Boston, MA 02111
(617) 542-3602
(617) 542-9103 (lawyer referral service)

MICHIGAN

State Bar of Michigan
306 Townsend Street
Lansing, MI 48933-2083
(517) 372-9030

http://www.michbar.org

MINNESOTA

Minnesota State Bar Association
514 Nicollet Mall
Minneapolis, MN 55402
(612) 333-1183

MISSISSIPPI

The Mississippi Bar
643 No. State Street
Jackson, Mississippi 39202
(601) 948-4471

MISSOURI

The Missouri Bar
P.O. Box 119, 326 Monroe
Jefferson City, Missouri 65102
(314) 635-4128

http://www.mobar.org

MONTANA

State Bar of Montana
46 North Main
PO Box 577
Helena, MT 59624
(406) 442-7660

NEBRASKA

Nebraska State Bar Association
635 South 14th Street, 2nd floor
Lincoln, NE 68508
(402) 475-7091

http://www.nebar.com

NEVADA

State Bar of Nevada
201 Las Vegas Blvd.
Las Vegas, NV 89101
(702) 382-2200

http://www.nvbar.org

NEW HAMPSHIRE

New Hampshire Bar Association
112 Pleasant Street
Concord, NH 03301
(603) 224-6942

NEW JERSEY

New Jersey State Bar Association
One Constitution Square
New Brunswuck, NJ 08901-1500
(908) 249-5000

NEW MEXICO

State Bar of New Mexico
121 Tijeras Street N.E.
Albuquerque, NM 87102

mailing address:
PO Box 25883
Albuquerque, NM 87125
(505) 843-6132

NEW YORK

New York State Bar Association
One Elk Street
Albany, NY 12207
(518) 463-3200

http://www.nysba.org

NORTH CAROLINA

North Carolina State Bar
208 Fayetteville Street Mall
Raleigh, NC 27601

mailing address:
PO Box 25908
Raleigh, NC 27611
(919) 828-4620

North Carolina Bar Association
1312 Annapolis Drive
Raleigh, NC 27608

mailing address:
PO Box 12806
Raleigh, NC 27605
(919) 828-0561

http://www.barlinc.org

NORTH DAKOTA

State Bar Association of North Dakota
515 1/2 East Broadway, suite 101
Bismarck, ND 58501

mailing address:
PO Box 2136
Bismarck, ND 58502
(701) 255-1404

OHIO

Ohio State Bar Association
1700 Lake Shore Drive
Columbus, OH 43204

mailing address:
PO Box 16562
Columbus, OH 43216-6562
(614) 487-2050

OKLAHOMA

Oklahoma Bar Association
1901 North Lincoln
Oklahoma City, OK 73105
(405) 524-2365

OREGON

Oregon State Bar
5200 S.W. Meadows Road
PO Box 1689
Lake Oswego, OR 97035-0889
(503) 620-0222

PENNSYLVANIA

Pennsylvannia Bar Association
100 South Street
PO Box 186
Harrisburg, PA 17108
(717) 238-6715

Pennsylvania Bar Institute
http://www.pbi.org

PUERTO RICO

Puerto Rico Bar Association
PO Box 1900
San Juan, Puerto Rico 00903
(809) 721-3358

RHODE ISLAND

Rhode Island Bar Association
115 Cedar Street
Providence, RI 02903
(401) 421-5740

SOUTH CAROLINA

South Carolina Bar
950 Taylor Street
PO Box 608
Columbia, SC 29202
(803) 799-6653

http://www.scbar.org

SOUTH DAKOTA

State Bar of South Dakota
222 East Capitol
Pierre, SD 57501
(605) 224-7554

TENNESSEE

Tennessee Bar Assn
3622 West End Avenue
Nashville, TN 37205
(615) 383-7421

http://www.tba.org

TEXAS

State Bar of Texas
1414 Colorado
PO Box 12487
Austin, TX 78711
(512) 463-1463

UTAH

Utah State Bar
645 South 200 East, Suite 310
Salt Lake City, UT 84111
(801) 531-9077

VERMONT

Vermont Bar Association
PO Box 100
Montpelier, VT 05601
(802) 223-2020

VIRGINIA

Virginia State Bar
707 East Main Street, suite 1500
Richmond, VA 23219-0501
(804) 775-0500

Virginia Bar Association
701 East Franklin St., Suite 1120
Richmond, VA 23219
(804) 644-0041

VIRGIN ISLANDS

Virgin Islands Bar Association
P.O. Box 4108
Christiansted, Virgin Islands
00822
(809) 778-7497

WASHINGTON

Washington State Bar
Association
500 Westin Street
2001 Sixth Avenue
Seattle, WA 98121-2599
(206) 727-8200

http://www.wsba.org

WEST VIRGINIA

West Virginia State Bar
2006 Kanawha Blvd. East
Charleston, WV 25311
(304) 558-2456

http://www.wvbar.org

West Virginia Bar Association
904 Security Building
100 Capitol Street
Charleston, WV 25301
(304) 342-1474

WISCONSIN

State Bar of Wisconsin
402 West Wilson Street
Madison, WI 53703
(608) 257-3838

http://www.wisbar.org/
home.htm

WYOMING

Wyoming State Bar
500 Randall Avenue
Cheyenne, WY 82001
PO Box 109
Cheyenne, WY 82003
(307) 632-9061

How to save on attorney fees

How to save on attorney fees

Millions of Americans know they need legal protection, whether it's to get agreements in writing, protect themselves from lawsuits, or document business transactions. But too often these basic but important legal matters are neglected because of something else millions of Americans know: legal services are expensive.

They don't have to be. In response to the demand for affordable legal protection and services, there are now specialized clinics that process simple documents. Paralegals help people prepare legal claims on a freelance basis. People find they can handle their own legal affairs with do-it-yourself legal guides and kits. Indeed, this book is a part of this growing trend.

When are these alternatives to a lawyer appropriate? If you hire an attorney, how can you make sure you're getting good advice for a reasonable fee? Most importantly, do you know how to lower your legal expenses?

When there is no alternative

Make no mistake: serious legal matters require a lawyer. The tips in this book can help you reduce your legal fees, but there is no alternative to good professional legal services in certain circumstances:

- when you are charged with a felony, you are a repeat offender, or jail is possible

- when a substantial amount of money or property is at stake in a lawsuit

- when you are a party in an adversarial divorce or custody case

- when you are an alien facing deportation

- when you are the plaintiff in a personal injury suit that involves large sums of money

- when you're involved in very important transactions

Are you sure you want to take it to court?

Consider the following questions before you pursue legal action:

What are your financial resources?

Money buys experienced attorneys, and experience wins over first-year lawyers and public defenders. Even with a strong case, you may save money by not going to court. Yes, people win millions in court. But for every big winner there are ten plaintiffs who either lose or win so little that litigation wasn't worth their effort.

Do you have the time and energy for a trial?

Courts are overbooked, and by the time your case is heard your initial zeal may have grown cold. If you can, make a reasonable settlement out of court. On personal matters, like a divorce or custody case, consider the emotional toll on all parties. Any legal case will affect you in some way. You will need time away from work. A newsworthy case may bring press coverage. Your loved ones, too, may face publicity. There is usually good reason to settle most cases quickly, quietly, and economically.

How can you settle disputes without litigation?

Consider *mediation*. In mediation, each party pays half the mediator's fee and, together, they attempt to work out a compromise informally. *Binding arbitration* is another alternative. For a small fee, a trained specialist serves as judge, hears both sides, and hands down a ruling that both parties have agreed to accept.

So you need an attorney

Having done your best to avoid litigation, if you still find yourself headed for court, you will need an attorney. To get the right attorney at a reasonable cost, be guided by these four questions:

What type of case is it?

You don't seek a foot doctor for a toothache. Find an attorney experienced in your type of legal problem. If you can get recommendations from clients who have recently won similar cases, do so.

Where will the trial be held?

You want a lawyer familiar with that court system and one who knows the court personnel and the local protocol—which can vary from one locality to another.

Should you hire a large or small firm?

Hiring a senior partner at a large and prestigious law firm sounds reassuring, but chances are the actual work will be handled by associates—at high rates. Small firms may give your case more attention but, with fewer resources, take longer to get the work done.

What can you afford?

Hire an attorney you can afford, of course, but know what a fee quote includes. High fees may reflect a firm's luxurious offices, high-paid staff and unmonitored expenses, while low estimates may mean "unexpected" costs later. Ask for a written estimate of all costs and anticipated expenses.

How to find a good lawyer

Whether you need an attorney quickly or you're simply open to future possibilities, here are seven nontraditional methods for finding your lawyer:

1) **Word of mouth**: Successful lawyers develop reputations. Your friends, business associates and other professionals are potential referral sources. But beware of hiring a friend. Keep the client-attorney relationship strictly business.

2) **Directories**: The Yellow Pages and the Martin-Hubbell Lawyer Directory (in your local library) can help you locate a lawyer with the right education, background and expertise for your case.

3) **Databases**: A paralegal should be able to run a quick computer search of local attorneys for you using the Westlaw or Lexis database.

4) **State bar associations**: Bar associations are listed in phone books. Along with lawyer referrals, your bar association can direct you to low-cost legal clinics or specialists in your area.

5) **Law schools**: Did you know that a legal clinic run by a law school gives law students hands-on experience? This may fit your legal needs. A third-year law student loaded with enthusiasm and a little experience might fill

the bill quite inexpensively—or even for free.

6) **Advertisements**: Ads are a lawyer's business card. If a "TV attorney" seems to have a good track record with your kind of case, why not call? Just don't be swayed by the glamour of a high-profile attorney.

7) **Your own ad**: A small ad describing the qualifications and legal expertise you're seeking, placed in a local bar association journal, may get you just the lead you need.

How to hire and work with your attorney

No matter how you hear about an attorney, you must interview him or her in person. Call the office during business hours and ask to speak to the attorney directly. Then explain your case briefly and mention how you obtained the attorney's name. If the attorney sounds interested and knowledgeable, arrange for a visit.

The ten-point visit

1) Note the address. This is a good indication of the rates to expect.

2) Note the condition of the offices. File-laden desks and poorly maintained work space may indicate a poorly run firm.

3) Look for up-to-date computer equipment and an adequate complement of support personnel.

4) Note the appearance of the attorney. How will he or she impress a judge or jury?

5) Is the attorney attentive? Does the attorney take notes, ask questions,

follow up on points you've mentioned?

6) Ask what schools he or she has graduated from, and feel free to check credentials with the state bar association.

7) Does the attorney have a good track record with your type of case?

8) Does he or she explain legal terms to you in plain English?

9) Are the firm's costs reasonable?

10) Will the attorney provide references?

Hiring the attorney

Having chosen your attorney, make sure all the terms are agreeable. Send letters to any other attorneys you have interviewed, thanking them for their time and interest in your case and explaining that you have retained another attorney's services.

Request a letter from your new attorney outlining your retainer agreement. The letter should list all fees you will be responsible for as well as the billing arrangement. Did you arrange to pay in installments? This should be noted in your retainer agreement.

Controlling legal costs

Legal fees and expenses can get out of control easily, but the client who is willing to put in the effort can keep legal costs manageable. Work out a budget with your attorney. Create a timeline for your case. Estimate the costs involved in each step.

Legal fees can be straightforward. Some lawyers charge a fixed rate for a specific project. Others charge contingency fees (they collect a percentage of your recovery, usually 35-50 percent if you win and nothing if you lose). But most attorneys prefer to bill by the hour. Expenses can run the gamut, with one hourly charge for taking depositions and another for making copies.

Have your attorney give you a list of charges for services rendered and an itemized monthly bill. The bill should explain the service performed, who performed the work, when the service was provided, how long it took, and how the service benefits your case.

Ample opportunity abounds in legal billing for dishonesty and greed. There is also plenty of opportunity for knowledgeable clients to cut their bills significantly if they know what to look for. Asking the right questions and setting limits on fees is smart and can save you a bundle. Don't be afraid to question legal bills. It's your case and your money!

When the bill arrives

- **Retainer fees**: You should already have a written retainer agreement. Ideally, the retainer fee applies toward case costs, and your agreement puts that in writing. Protect yourself by escrowing the retainer fee until the case has been handled to your satisfaction.

- **Office visit charges**: Track your case and all documents, correspondence, and bills. Diary all dates, deadlines and questions you want to ask your attorney during your next office visit. This keeps expensive office visits focused and productive, with more accomplished in less time. If your attorney charges less for phone consultations than office visits, reserve visits for those tasks that must be done in person.

- **Phone bills**: This is where itemized bills are essential. Who made the call, who was spoken to, what was discussed, when was the call made, and how long did it last? Question any charges that seem unnecessary or excessive (over 60 minutes).

- **Administrative costs**: Your case may involve hundreds, if not thousands, of documents: motions, affidavits, depositions, interrogatories, bills, memoranda, and letters. Are they all necessary? Understand your attorney's case strategy before paying for an endless stream of costly documents.

- **Associate and paralegal fees**: Note in your retainer agreement which staff people will have access to your file. Then you'll have an informed and efficient staff working on your case, and you'll recognize their names on your bill. Of course, your attorney should handle the important part of your case, but less costly paralegals or associates may handle routine matters more economically. Note: Some firms expect their associates to meet a quota of billable hours, although the time spent is not always warranted. Review your bill. Does the time spent make sense for the document in question? Are several staff involved in matters that should be handled by one person? Don't be afraid to ask questions. And withhold payment until you have satisfactory answers.

- **Court stenographer fees**: Depositions and court hearings require costly transcripts and stenographers. This means added expenses. Keep an eye on these costs.

- **Copying charges**: Your retainer fee should limit the number of copies made of your complete file. This is in your legal interest, because multiple files mean multiple chances others may access your confidential information. It is also in your financial interest, because copying costs can be astronomical.

- **Fax costs**: As with the phone and copier, the fax can easily run up costs. Set a limit.

- **Postage charges**: Be aware of how much it costs to send a legal document overnight, or a registered letter. Offer to pick up or deliver expensive items when it makes sense.

- **Filing fees**: Make it clear to your attorney that you want to minimize the number of court filings in your case. Watch your bill and question any filing that seems unnecessary.

- **Document production fee**: Turning over documents to your opponent is mandatory and expensive. If you're faced with reproducing boxes of documents, consider having the job done by a commercial firm rather than your attorney's office.

- **Research and investigations**: Pay only for photographs that can be used in court. Can you hire a photographer at a lower rate than what your attorney charges? Reserve that right in your retainer agreement. Database research can also be extensive and expensive; if your attorney uses Westlaw or Nexis, set limits on the research you will pay for.

- **Expert witnesses**: Question your attorney if you are expected to pay for more than a reasonable number of expert witnesses. Limit the number to what is essential to your case.

- **Technology costs**: Avoid videos, tape recordings, and graphics if you can use old-fashioned diagrams to illustrate your case.

- **Travel expenses**: Travel expenses for those connected to your case can be quite costly unless you set a maximum budget. Check all travel-related items on your bill, and make sure they are appropriate. Always question why the travel is necessary before you agree to pay for it.

- **Appeals costs**: Losing a case often means an appeal, but weigh the costs involved before you make that decision. If money is at stake, do a cost-benefit analysis to see if an appeal is financially justified.

- **Monetary damages**: Your attorney should be able to help you estimate the total damages you will have to pay if you lose a civil case. Always consider settling out of court rather than proceeding to trial when the trial costs will be high.

- **Surprise costs**: Surprise costs are so routine they're predictable. The judge may impose unexpected court orders on one or both sides, or the opposition will file an unexpected motion that increases your legal costs. Budget a few

157

thousand dollars over what you estimate your case will cost. It usually is needed.

- **Padded expenses**: Assume your costs and expenses are legitimate. But some firms do inflate expenses—office supplies, database searches, copying, postage, phone bills—to bolster their bottom line. Request copies of bills your law firm receives from support services. If you are not the only client represented on a bill, determine those charges related to your case.

Keeping it legal without a lawyer

The best way to save legal costs is to avoid legal problems. There are hundreds of ways to decrease your chances of lawsuits and other nasty legal encounters. Most simply involve a little common sense. You can also use your own initiative to find and use the variety of self-help legal aid available to consumers.

11 situations in which you may not need a lawyer

1) **No-fault divorce**: Married couples with no children, minimal property, and no demands for alimony can take advantage of divorce mediation services. A lawyer should review your divorce agreement before you sign it, but you will have saved a fortune in attorney fees. A marital or family counselor may save a seemingly doomed marriage, or help both parties move beyond anger to a calm settlement. Either way, counseling can save you money.

2) **Wills**: Do-it-yourself wills and living trusts are ideal for people with estates of less than $600,000. Even if an attorney reviews your final documents, a will kit allows you to read the documents, ponder your bequests, fill out sample forms, and discuss your wishes with your family at your leisure,

without a lawyer's meter running.

3) **Incorporating**: Incorporating a small business can be done by any business owner. Your state government office provides the forms and instructions necessary. A visit to your state office will probably be necessary to perform a business name check. A fee of $100-$200 is usually charged for processing your Articles of Incorporation. The rest is paperwork: filling out forms correctly; holding regular, official meetings; and maintaining accurate records.

4) **Routine business transactions**: Copyrights, for example, can be applied for by asking the U.S. Copyright Office for the appropriate forms and brochures. The same is true of the U.S. Patent and Trademark Office. If your business does a great deal of document preparation and research, hire a certified paralegal rather than paying an attorney's rates. Consider mediation or binding arbitration rather than going to court for a business dispute. Hire a human resources/benefits administrator to head off disputes concerning discrimination or other employee charges.

5) **Repairing bad credit**: When money matters get out of hand, attorneys and bankruptcy should not be your first solution. Contact a credit counseling organization that will help you work out manageable payment plans so that everyone wins. It can also help you learn to manage your money better. A good company to start with is the Consumer Credit Counseling Service, 1-800-388-2227.

6) **Small Claims Court**: For legal grievances amounting to a few thousand dollars in damages, represent yourself in Small Claims Court. There is a small filing fee, forms to fill out, and several court visits necessary. If you can collect evidence, state your case in a clear and logical presentation, and come across as neat, respectful and sincere, you can succeed in Small Claims Court.

7) **Traffic Court**: Like Small Claims Court, Traffic Court may show more compassion to a defendant appearing without an attorney. If you are

ticketed for a minor offense and want to take it to court, you will be asked to plead guilty or not guilty. If you plead guilty, you can ask for leniency in sentencing by presenting mitigating circumstances. Bring any witnesses who can support your story, and remember that presentation (some would call it acting ability) is as important as fact.

8) **Residential zoning petition**: If a homeowner wants to open a home business, build an addition, or make other changes that may affect his or her neighborhood, town approval is required. But you don't need a lawyer to fill out a zoning variance application, turn it in, and present your story at a public hearing. Getting local support before the hearing is the best way to assure a positive vote; contact as many neighbors as possible to reassure them that your plans won't adversely affect them or the neighborhood.

9) **Government benefit applications**: Applying for veterans' or unemployment benefits may be daunting, but the process doesn't require legal help. Apply for either immediately upon becoming eligible. Note: If your former employer contests your application for unemployment benefits and you have to defend yourself at a hearing, you may want to consider hiring an attorney.

10) **Receiving government files**: The Freedom of Information Act gives every American the right to receive copies of government information about him or her. Write a letter to the appropriate state or federal agency, noting the precise information you want. List each document in a separate paragraph. Mention the Freedom of Information Act, and state that you will pay any expenses. Close with your signature and the address the documents should be sent to. An approved request may take six months to arrive. If it is refused on the grounds that the information is classified or violates another's privacy, send a letter of appeal explaining why the released information would not endanger anyone. Enlist the support of your local state or federal representative, if possible, to smooth the approval process.

11) **Citizenship**:Arriving in the United States to work and become a citizen is a process tangled in bureaucratic red tape, but it requires more perseverance than legal assistance. Immigrants can learn how to obtain a "Green Card," under what circumstances they can work, and what the requirements of citizenship are by contacting the Immigration Services or reading a good self-help book.

Save more; it's E-Z

When it comes to saving attorneys' fees, E-Z Legal Forms is the consumer's best friend. America's largest publisher of self-help legal products offers legally valid forms for virtually every situation. E-Z Legal Kits and E-Z Legal Made E-Z Guides include all necessary forms with a simple-to-follow manual of instructions or a layman's book. E-Z Legal Books are a legal library of forms and documents for everyday business and personal needs. E-Z Legal Software provides those same forms on disk and CD for customized documents at the touch of the keyboard.

You can add to your legal savvy and your ability to protect yourself, your loved ones, your business and your property with a range of self-help legal titles available through E-Z Legal Forms. See the product descriptions and information at the back of this guide.

Save On Legal Fees

with software and books from E-Z Legal available at your
nearest bookstore, or call 1-800-822-4566

Stock No.: LA101
$24.95 8.5" x 11"
500 pages Soft cover
ISBN 1-56382-101-X

Everyday Law Made E-Z

The book that saves legal fees every time it's opened.

Here, in *Everyday Law Made E-Z*, are fast answers to 90% of the legal
questions anyone is ever likely to ask, such as:

- How can I control my neighbor's pet?
- Can I change my name?
- What is a common law marriage?
- When should I incorporate my business?
- Is a child responsible for his bills?
- Who owns a husband's gifts to his wife?
- How do I become a naturalized citizen?
- Should I get my divorce in Nevada?
- Can I write my own will?
- Who is responsible when my son drives my car?
- How can my uncle get a Green Card?
- What are the rights of a non-smoker?
- Do I have to let the police search my car?
- What is sexual harassment?
- When is euthanasia legal?
- What repairs must my landlord make?
- What's the difference between fair criticism and slander?
- When can I get my deposit back?
- Can I sue the federal government?
- Am I responsible for a drunken guest's auto accident?
- Is a hotel liable if it does not honor a reservation?
- Does my car fit the lemon law?

Whether for personal or business use, this 500-page information-packed book
helps the layman safeguard his property, avoid disputes, comply with legal
obligations, and enforce his rights. Hundreds of cases illustrate thousands of
points of law, each clearly and completely explained.

E·Z LEGAL BOOKS®

Turn your computer into your personal lawyer

The E-Z Way to SAVE TIME and MONEY!
Print professional forms from your computer in minutes!

Only $29.⁹⁵ each!

Everyday Legal Forms & Agreements Made E-Z
A complete library of 301 legal documents for virtually every business or personal situation—at your fingertips!

Item No. CD311

Credit Repair Made E-Z
Our proven formula for obtaining your credit report, removing the negative marks, and establishing "Triple A" credit!

Item No. SW1103

Corporate Record Keeping Made E-Z
Essential for every corporation in America. Keep records in compliance with over 170 standard minutes, notices and resolutions.

Item No. CD314

Divorce Law Made E-Z
Couples seeking an uncontested divorce can save costly lawyers' fees by filing the forms themselves.

Item No. SW1102

Incorporation Made E-Z
We provide all the information you need to protect your personal assets from business creditors...without a lawyer.

Item No. SW1101

Living Trusts Made E-Z
Take steps now to avoid costly, time-consuming probate and eliminate one more worry for your family by creating your own revocable living trust.

Item No. SW1105

Managing Employees Made E-Z
Manage employees efficiently, effectively and legally with 246 forms, letters and memos covering everything from hiring to firing.

Item No. CD312

Last Wills Made E-Z*
Ensure your property goes to the heirs you choose. Includes Living Will and Power of Attorney for Healthcare forms for each state.

Item No. SW1107

ss 1999.r1

BE INFORMED — PROTECTED!

The E-Z Legal Sexual Harassment Poster

If you do not have a well-communicated sexual harassment policy, you are vulnerable to employee lawsuits for sexual harassment.

Give your employees the information they need and protect your company from needless harassment suits by placing this poster wherever you hang your labor law poster.

BONUS! Receive our helpful manual *How to Avoid Sexual Harassment Lawsuits* with your purchase of the Sexual Harassment Poster.

See the order form in this guide, and order yours today!

FEDERAL & STATE
Labor Law Posters

State	Item#	State	Item#	State	Item#
Alabama	83801	Louisiana	83818	Ohio	83835
Alaska	83802	Maine	83819	Oklahoma	83836
Arizona	83803	Maryland	83820	Oregon	83837
Arkansas	83804	Massachusetts	83821	Pennsylvania	83838
California	83805	Michigan	83822	Rhode Island	83839
Colorado	83806	Minnesota	83823	South Carolina	83840
Connecticut	83807	Mississippi	83824	South Dakota not available	
Delaware	83808	Missouri	83825	Tennessee	83842
Florida	83809	Montana	83826	Texas	83843
Georgia	83810	Nebraska	83827	Utah	83844
Hawaii	83811	Nevada	83828	Vermont	83845
Idaho	83812	New Hampshire	83829	Virginia	83846
Illinois	83813	New Jersey	83830	Washington	83847
Indiana	83814	New Mexico	83831	Washington, D.C.	83848
Iowa	83815	New York	83832	West Virginia	83849
Kansas	83816	North Carolina	83833	Wisconsin	83850
Kentucky	83817	North Dakota	83834	Wyoming	83851

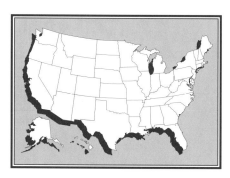

State Labor Law Compliance Poster
Avoid up to $10,000 in fines by posting the required State Labor Law Poster available from E-Z Legal.

$29.95

Federal Labor Law Poster
This colorful, durable 17³/₄" x 24" poster is in full federal compliance and includes:

* The NEW Fair Labor Standards Act Effective October 1, 1996 (New Minimum Wage Act)

* The Family & Medical Leave Act of 1993*

* The Occupational Safety and Health Protection Act of 1970

* The Equal Opportunity Act

* The Employee Polygraph Protection Act

* Businesses with fewer than 50 employees should display reverse side of poster, which excludes this act.

$11.99
Stock No. LP001

ss1999.r1

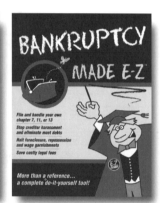

Index